D0554836

FACULTY DEVELOPMENT
AND STUDENT LEARNING

SCHOLARSHIP OF TEACHING AND LEARNING

Editors
Jennifer Meta Robinson
Whitney M. Schlegel
Mary Taylor Huber
Pat Hutchings

FACULTY DEVELOPMENT AND STUDENT LEARNING

Assessing the Connections

William Condon, Ellen R. Iverson,
Cathryn A. Manduca, Carol Rutz,
and Gudrun Willett

Foreword by Mary Taylor Huber
Afterword by Richard Haswell

Indiana University Press

Bloomington and Indianapolis

This book is a publication of

Indiana University Press
Office of Scholarly Publishing
Herman B Wells Library 350
1320 East 10th Street
Bloomington, Indiana 47405 USA

iupress.indiana.edu

© 2016 by William Condon, Ellen R. Iverson, Cathryn A. Manduca, Carol Rutz, and Gudrun Willett

Manufactured in the United States of America

Cataloging information is available from the Library of Congress

ISBN 978-0-253-01878-6 (cloth)
ISBN 978-0-253-01886-1 (ebook)

1 2 3 4 5 21 20 19 18 17 16

Contents

Foreword

Pathways from Faculty Learning to Student Learning and Beyond

Mary Taylor Huber

One of the questions many of us are often asked is whether engagement in the scholarship of teaching and learning leads to improvements in student learning. How do/would you answer this question? What would you point to as evidence for this connection on your campus?[1]

Ask a question like this to directors of faculty development programs of any kind and you will likely find what my colleagues and I found among leaders of campus initiatives to support the scholarship of teaching and learning: "puzzlement and frustration over the difficulties of documentation." (Hutchings, Huber, and Ciccone 2011, 137)

Faculty Development and Student Learning: Assessing the Connections provides a model for mapping this treacherous territory, where so many educators fear to tread. The authors, a multidisciplinary team from Carleton College, the Science Education Resource Center (SERC) at Carleton, and Washington State University (WSU), trace the effects on their two campuses of initiatives that have encouraged faculty to look closely and critically at student learning as a way to improve instruction in writing, critical thinking, and quantitative reasoning. I have been privileged to serve as an advisor to the "Tracer Project" (as it is known) since 2008, joining the authors in conversation as they sought ways to answer hard, puzzling questions about whether well-designed faculty development programs actually change participants' approaches to teaching, improve the quality of student work produced in those classrooms, and contribute to a more generative and productive culture of teaching and learning on campus.

The challenges of documenting connections between faculty learning and student learning are, famously, legion. It's one thing to engage faculty in programs that invite classroom inquiry and innovation, as many faculty development programs do. But it's another thing to show that faculty actually make changes in their teaching as a result of that engagement, that these pedagogical innovations (new goals, activities, assessments, etc.) in turn lead to changes in student learning, and that all of these changes are in fact improvements! This is a tall order, hard enough to show case by case. But what happens over time? Do participants continue to innovate in later offerings of their course, or in other courses they teach? And what happens elsewhere on campus? Do colleagues learn from each other? Do expectations rise on campus for what is possible and desirable for teachers to do?

These questions are as important as they are difficult to answer. Higher education is awash in initiatives that encourage faculty to adopt "evidence-based" teaching practices. But what evidence do we have that these initiatives will translate into the promised learning improvements? Research may have shown that "evidence-based" practices, such as active forms of instruction in the sciences (Freeman et al. 2014) or "high impact practices" (Kuh 2008), can work well in a number of different disciplines, class sizes, or institutional settings. But can they do so on one's own campus? How well do these practices travel from the workshops where they are introduced, to participants' own classrooms and to their students' learning?

The scholarship of teaching and learning (SoTL) provides a useful case in point. SoTL practitioners ask questions about student learning in their classrooms or programs, gather and analyze evidence to help answer those questions, and try out new insights about learning in their pedagogy and course designs, and then make their findings public for colleagues to review, critique, and build upon. Campus programs to encourage SoTL typically provide small grants or fellowships for faculty to engage in this work; bring fellows together regularly to discuss relevant literature and exchange ideas; offer workshops on methods, research ethics, and so on; provide a venue for posters and presentations at the end of the fellowship period; and (often) support travel to conferences where fellows can engage with wider communities of colleagues.

Participants in such programs often report that the experience has been transformative for them as teachers; that gaining a better understanding of their students has encouraged them to change goals, assignments, and/or assessments; and that they have evidence that more of their students were doing better work as a result (Huber and Hutchings 2005; see also Voelker and Martin 2013). Yet what evidence do program directors have that supporting SoTL is a good investment for the campus or that it has led to improvements in student learning overall?

My colleagues and I asked about such connections in the survey mentioned at the start of this foreword, and fifty-two SoTL program directors wrote thoughtful replies. Many noted that improvements in student learning could be shown from individual projects, but to give a sense of the whole was much more difficult. Many could cite good reasons for why one might *expect* a positive effect ("more faculty spend more time and effort on teaching which might improve learning") but worried about the difficulties of demonstrating direct results. Indeed, some doubted that finding evidence for an effect on learning was possible ("I don't think there is a straight path from an intervention to improvement in student learning"). Several were, frankly, flummoxed: "This is a vexed question," one respondent said. "It is a major concern," wrote another.

And one noted, frankly, "We need help here" (see Huber, Hutchings, and Ciccone 2011, 136–137).

Faculty Development and Student Learning could not be timelier. Over the past twenty-five years or so, a shift in focus from teaching toward learning has energized a reform movement that encompasses many initiatives with similar goals. Whether aimed broadly at supporting faculty in the scholarship of teaching and learning or focused more closely on teaching for a particular learning goal, these programs are engaging ever larger numbers of educators across academic ranks and roles. The effects, accelerated by external pressures for accountability, have transformed college teaching from what was once a sleepy academic backwater into a buzzing hive of efforts to improve the learning experience for college students, increase rates of completion, and raise—and effectively measure—levels of achievement.

You can see evidence of this transformation in the growth of faculty development opportunities around the world. Training for graduate student teaching assistants has been on the rise, the numbers of faculty development centers have increased, their programming has become more comprehensive, and, in some countries, their courses for new faculty are even required. Campus centers now assist faculty in incorporating technology into the classroom and support instructors of freshman seminars. Programs offer pedagogies that involve students more deeply, assignments that elicit higher levels of learning and performance, and assessments that can better inform new course designs.

One might think that faculty development would be secure as a major priority on campuses that are eager to take advantage of the many new possibilities for teaching and learning available today. But, sadly, that is not always the case. Because money is tight and institutional success is often tied to more visible priorities than pedagogy, funding for faculty development and other supports for teaching innovation remains vulnerable. Indeed, one of the guiding questions for the authors of *Faculty Development and Student Learning* has been how best to show that faculty learning in such programs advances goals that institutions value, and thus provide evidence that investment in faculty development is worthwhile. Programs that support the scholarship of teaching and learning would certainly benefit, but so too would other initiatives that share SoTL's commitment to learning about learning as a route to better educational experiences and outcomes for college students.

The interest of this book for scholars of teaching and learning goes well beyond the help it can offer to those who wish to explore and document the effects of SoTL-friendly faculty development programs. Just as important are the study's findings about the pathways through which faculty learning can enrich the culture of teaching on a campus, contributing to a context in which innovative teaching is welcomed (even expected) and scholarly teaching can thrive. As my colleagues and I argued in *The Scholarship of Teaching and Learning Reconsidered*, SoTL advocates have long aspired to see this work "take hold at a deep level of institutional 'incorporation,'" so that "teaching is understood as intellectual work; that it is, indeed, 'work' in the richest, most generative sense of the word; that it can be improved through inquiry and investigation; and that it's a fit and proper subject for exchange with colleagues who just might be interested themselves, or doing related work and eager to learn from the experience of others" (Hutchings, Huber, and Ciccone 2011, 112). The Tracer Project helps us see how formal faculty development can interact with other sites of faculty learning and contribute to this larger effect.

Indeed, this study was conducted as a kind of SoTL inquiry itself. To be sure, it is not a classic practitioner study of teaching and learning in a particular course or academic program. As the authors argue, however, well-designed faculty development programs function as curricula with specific goals and potentially measurable outcomes. From this perspective, the Tracer team can be understood as practitioner researchers using a variety of methods to probe the effects of their curricula on the learning of participating faculty, their students, and their colleagues—or, to put it another way, on its contributions to teaching, learning, and the culture of teaching on campus.

It is also worth underlining the Tracer Project's careful attention to contextualized evidence for learning (both faculty's and students'), and the multiple methods they have used to help them see more clearly the kinds of learning they most cared about. In short, the research team did what scholars of teaching and learning usually do: they talked to the learners (faculty) who had participated in these programs and gathered and analyzed evidence for their learning in their syllabi, assignments, and (in one line of inquiry) classroom observation. On the undergraduate side, the Tracer team looked for evidence in the work that students produced in these teachers' courses, measured by rubrics relevant to each site's learning goals. Readers will see that the Tracer team also followed that arc of inquiry along which many scholars of teaching and learning have traveled, beginning with "what works" questions but moving on to more fundamental inquiries about "what's going on" now and "what's possible" in the future (Hutchings 2000).

In regard to "what works," *Faculty Development and Student Learning* reports some good news. Briefly put, the work suggests that, yes, well-designed faculty development programs can contribute to teaching in ways that elicit better student work around core institutional learning goals. More precisely, they found that at both institutions, such programs can lead faculty toward a new view of teaching and learning, resulting in continuing classroom improvement efforts that appear to have correlates in improved student learning. Indeed, the evidence at both schools suggests that students of faculty who engage in multiple opportunities for learning about teaching produce better work when compared with students of faculty who are low-participators in faculty development.

The Tracer team's conclusion about "what's going on" is that good pedagogical ideas are effective, sticky, and generative, a finding that speaks to how these pedagogical ideas travel and spread. Right now, at Washington State University, teaching remains (as the authors puts it) an "activity of the left hand." Yet even there, opportunities for talking about teaching and learning have become more common. Indeed, the research team had trouble finding people who had *not* participated in some form of learning about teaching—largely because, driven by accreditation, all departments are now expected to identify student learning outcomes, assess them, and make changes in order to address weaknesses. At WSU, it's not at the institutional level so much as in particular departments, where richer cultures of teaching are developing.

If one wants a picture of what's going on at the institutional level, the Tracer teams' three-year ethnography at Carleton College illuminates how a much more public, college-wide culture of teaching has developed there over the past fifteen or twenty years. It's not just in pockets but is broadly based, and has "thickened" the social life around teaching and learning considerably—even in a college where expectations for research productivity are extremely high. This broadens the range of motivation for participation in faculty development, multiplies the kinds of occasions in which these issues are normal topics of discussion, and expands the channels through which new ideas and new attitudes toward teaching and learning flow.

And this leads to the team's larger questions about "what's possible," drawing attention to the potential that initiatives like these have for contributing to the development of more robust departmental and institutional cultures of teaching and learning. By creating new and better forums for pedagogical conversation and inquiry about learning, faculty development programs on these campuses are contributing, as the Tracer authors suggest, "to the formation of an informed, agile professoriate that adapts and improves teaching in response to new ideas or challenges."

Three messages stand out to me from *Faculty Development and Student Learning*. First, and probably most important, is that well-designed faculty development initiatives can contribute to teaching in ways that elicit better student work around core institutional learning goals. Another may be that it's possible to show this! And a third is that faculty development can also contribute to a more public face for teaching and learning, a transformative shift toward looking at learning from a student's perspective, and a view of teaching as a field of knowledge and practice that improves and grows.

FACULTY DEVELOPMENT AND STUDENT LEARNING

1 Connecting Faculty Learning to Student Learning

THE RELATIONSHIP BETWEEN teaching and learning is fundamental to higher education. The premise of higher education is that teaching by highly educated individuals engaged in ongoing learning of their own produces a valuable opportunity for students to learn essential knowledge and skills that will prepare them for life and career. This book's title captures some reigning buzzwords in higher education: faculty development, student learning, and assessment—words that describe pieces of the puzzle of understanding and improving the relationship between teaching and learning. The research reported in this book demonstrates that these common terms belong together through evidence from two distinctly different institutions gathered over three years through a mixed-methods study. Unpacking these anodyne terms may be useful.

If any programmatic term is likely to induce a wince, surely it would be "faculty development." Faculty themselves tend to read the term as an indication of shortcomings that require attention and active correction. While administrators recognize that faculty are employees first and need some orientation to a new workplace, it may be difficult to justify spending resources on additional opportunities for faculty highly qualified to manage learning within their disciplines to learn about teaching. Students may praise or complain about individual faculty, yet they seem to grant faculty expertise and professionalism. The notion that faculty should apply the lifelong learning that they advocate for students to the professional practice of teaching may not register.

"Assessment" attempts to map learning gains onto the curriculum and, in some cases, the co-curriculum, to show how students benefit from instruction and skills practice during their college careers. Attention from accreditors and state legislatures has raised the stakes for many institutions, demanding not just valid assessment measures, but continuous improvement in student learning based on findings.

"Student learning" would be the heart of any educational institution's mission, applicable to the curriculum and the co-curriculum, with the goal of providing an education for persons who aspire to post-graduate lives as citizens, workers, leaders, and family members. Measures of student learning, from course grades to assessment instruments such as surveys, portfolios, and barrier exams, speak to classroom experiences parsed in units of terms, years, and graduation requirements.

The three terms tend to march in pairs, with student learning as a kind of fulcrum: *faculty development,* understood in the scholarship of teaching and learning (SoTL) sense, offers teaching faculty opportunities to learn new approaches, technologies, and more. As a result, faculty apply their new learning to the classroom in a research mode, aiming to improve *student learning. Student learning,* however, pairs more neatly with *assessment,* divorcing statistical findings from the classroom experiences informed by faculty members' growing knowledge and professional development. Integrating *faculty development* and *student learning* requires *assessment* of both kinds of teaching and learning. How do faculty use the learning they acquire through development activities to improve their teaching? As teaching improves, does student learning also improve?

Through an extensive mixed-methods study conducted on two campuses, Carleton College and Washington State University, this study traces (hence the nickname Tracer Project) the effects of faculty development into students' learning through course work products and, more generally, into the institutional culture that supports a teaching community. This research supports the goal of understanding the relationship between faculty development, teaching practice, and student learning with findings that show clearly that faculty want to improve their teaching, take advantage of institutional opportunities to do so, and strive to change their teaching to deliver better learning opportunities to their students.

Some of the Tracer Project's findings confirm existing research in SoTL. For example, one important reason that colleges and universities provide teacher development programming is that, for the most part, people who become college faculty learn far more about teaching as in-service teachers than they do as pre-service graduate students (Austin, Connolly, and Colbeck 2008)—if for no other reason than they are faculty far longer than they are graduate students. Existing studies also reveal ways that faculty development affects teaching practices: those who take advantage of development opportunities report changing their classroom approaches as well as assignment and course designs (Gibbs and Coffey 2004; Austin, Connolly, and Colbeck 2008; Fishman et al. 2003; Loucks-Horsley et al. 2003; Garet et al. 2001). Whether or how such changes affect students' learning is not necessarily clear from these studies. Some studies indicate that teaching approaches can influence students' interest and in turn their learning (Pressick-Kilborn and Walker 2002; Hidi and Renninger 2006): the Tracer Project sought more direct evidence of improvements in student's learning outcomes—in their work products. Without such key information faculty development programs remain vulnerable, tentative, even ephemeral at many, if not most, colleges and universities.

Seeking an answer to whether improving faculty members' teaching practices leads to improved students' learning leads to analyzing institutional actions and conditions that promote faculty development, reflective teaching practices, and identifying and promulgating best practices in the classroom. An understanding of effective teaching in higher education must also include a view of faculty learning, institutional conditions that encourage and support it, and its effects on students. Higher education as a whole must understand how students' learning is affected by faculty members' efforts to become better teachers and how faculty members, in their efforts to become better teachers, might make common cause, thus promulgating a visibly positive culture of teaching and learning on their campuses. In doing so, taking a holistic view is important not only because it promotes a systemic approach to improving teaching and learning but also because it renders a better picture of the faculty learning process itself (Wayne, Yoon, Zhu, Cronen, and Garet 2008).

A metaphor for the resulting structure is a kind of dual spiral—not a double helix, but two separate intertwined spirals, one of which represents an individual faculty member's experience and learning and a second that stands for what faculty members working together might produce in the way of community learning—a community of practice, perhaps, or a productive culture of teaching and learning. The individual's spiral takes account of the iterative nature of teaching in higher education. Faculty members tend to teach the same set of courses repeatedly over time. In olden times, the figure of the white-haired scholar with his yellowed lecture notes that never changed from term to term provided a visual for that iterative process. However, faculty who work on their teaching develop assignments and other assessment techniques that help them understand how well students are learning; and so from iteration to iteration, teachers learn how to make the course more effective for students. Thus, rather than circling back to the beginning point, the knowledge gained from the previous iterations results in beginning at a new, more informed point—the motion is more like a spiral. The collective spiral may begin at a particular point—a faculty development effort, a SoTL self-study, a department's goal-setting session, an institutional review of its mission—and open up its radius and its influence over time, as the emerging new culture adds knowledge to everyone's teaching. Both spirals are self-contained yet remain open to new influences, and the latter one freely accommodates additional participants.

When considering connections between faculty learning, teaching, and student learning, higher education must own a collective image problem: faculty and administrators are perceived as not caring about teaching. Supportive, effective cultures of teaching and learning are rarely obvious, perhaps because faculty members' efforts to improve their teaching are simply not as visible as other areas of their work (Beyer, Taylor, and Gillmore 2013; Shulman 1993). Three recent books that, curiously, both attack and support higher education all aim to reform the academy's practices. All three focus substantially on the need to improve student learning outcomes, and all three—ally and adversary alike—operate from the unsupported assumption that faculty care less about teaching than about other aspects of their jobs—primarily research. Arum and Roksa's *Academically Adrift* (2011) identifies a lack of attention to or ability for teaching as a major reason for deficiencies in student learning across the academy. However, their assertions about how faculty devalue teaching are grounded in data that actually show the opposite—that students' gains on a very general instrument such as the Collegiate Learning Assessment are consistent and occur across all categories the authors analyzed (Haswell 2012). These assumptions are just that—assumptions. They are, in rhetorical terms, commonplaces, accepted by the audience as part of what everyone knows. Everyone "knows" that faculty are rewarded for research; hence, everyone "knows" that faculty don't care about teaching. Two more recent volumes, *College: What It Was, Is, and Should Be* (Delbanco 2012) and *We're Losing Our Minds: Rethinking American Higher Education* (Keeling and Hersh 2012), provide a similar attack, but from within. Keeling and Hersh bemoan the "absence of a serious culture of teaching and learning, and the consequent insufficient quality and quantity of student learning" (175). Delbanco chimes in that "our colleges and universities are failing to deliver true higher learning" and that "learning is no longer the first priority of our university" (1). According to both books, faculty who care more about research than about teaching play a major role in the decline. In both, too, no evidence is offered to support the assumption that faculty do not value teaching: that "truth" is simply asserted.

That such a commonplace persists in spite of research to the contrary is cause for alarm—and a call for further research about teaching and learning. It is tempting to counter such attacks before carefully examining the aspects of the commonplace that seem true. In fact, most who teach in higher education can identify examples of the stereotype—though for a number of reasons, the stereotype is becoming rarer and rarer—and perhaps it exists most prominently in the kinds of institution on which Arum and Roksa, Keeling and Hirsh, and Delbanco focus: the elite, international research universities that *do* feature prominently in their mission the investigation into new knowledge. At some institutions—and for some faculty at most institutions—the focus on research can overtake the focus on teaching, particularly when research funding results in supplanting teaching responsibilities (Fairweather and Beach 2002). However, for most higher education faculty, the classroom remains a major focus. For some years, surveys of college faculty have revealed that even at research universities—where the requirements for research are greatest and therefore most in conflict with teaching duties—the majority of faculty spend over a quarter of their time preparing for teaching and another quarter of their time in scheduled teaching (Eagan et al. 2014). Faculty cannot easily ignore or neglect an activity that occupies almost half their time and attention. So in one way or another, faculty do learn to become better teachers. Some learn through formal events that focus on improving teaching—the equivalent of in-service training. Huber and Hutchings (2005), however, remind the academy that "the knowledge needed for teaching is often deeply contextual and tied closely to the details of classroom practice" (122). Teachers mine their practices and those of their colleagues as they learn. In other words, improvement happens via individual, intentional actions that affect teaching incrementally, over time. Finally, faculty receive feedback on the quality of their teaching at many points in their professional lives; hiring practices, annual reviews, and the tenure and promotion process, to mention but a few, all provide high-stakes evaluation and feedback on teaching. Still, the fact that many are so ready to believe the commonplace that college faculty do not care about teaching—even among college and university faculty—is a problem that needs to be examined with data rather than mere assumptions.

When faculty learn more about teaching, logic dictates that they become better teachers; and when faculty become better teachers, their students learn more or experience better learning. Faculty should be able to respond more effectively to the ever-changing demands of the classroom if they are (1) well informed by educational and learning research; (2) learn what is working (and not) in their own and others' classrooms; and (3) have iterative opportunities to learn, practice, and reflect upon a repertoire of teaching strategies and skills. Faculty learning encompasses three sites for improving teaching:

1. Formal faculty development activities such as workshops, brown bags, professional conferences, or colloquia;

2. Intentional, self-directed efforts to examine and improve one's own teaching, as seen in the SoTL movement and in other research that considers the independent actions faculty take to improve their teaching (Beyer, Taylor, and Gillmore 2013; Handelsman et al. 2004; Mettetal 2001; Kember 2002); and

3. Routine events—annual reviews, hiring processes, departmental goal setting— that are by no means intended as sites for learning about teaching but that carry incidental opportunities to do so, if institutions learn to take advantage of those opportunities.

The challenge is to trace the effects of those developmental opportunities into the classroom and from there into student learning.

Formal Faculty Development

This book outlines questions, methods, and findings that begin to untangle this fascinating chain of learning relationships—for teachers as well as students. In terms of traditional faculty development—intentional, in-service activities overtly planned to improve various aspects of teaching performance—the study produced evidence that faculty who participate in professional development activities do alter classroom pedagogy in ways congruent with the development. Thus, faculty who most evidently do care about their teaching make a point to join in a collective effort to improve teaching and learning, and those efforts pay off at least in how participating faculty design courses and assignments, how they employ new technologies in their teaching, how they respond to and evaluate students' learning, and in many other ways. The subsequent effects on student learning are clearly more difficult to trace, due to a host of confounding variables. Nonetheless, the study produced tantalizing results obtained from mixed-methods research on the two campuses. However, the greatest effects concern the aggregate impact of multiple professional development experiences and the varied interactions they generate among instructors on a campus. The study shows that these effects are large, extend beyond the participants in formal faculty development programs, and guide an institutional culture that supports reflective, scholarly teaching. This generative culture of teaching and learning provides the crucial environment for ongoing faculty learning that benefits students, faculty, and the institution as a whole.

Additionally, for those who care to look for it, the evidence for faculty engagement in improving teaching is already clear. Faculty development is already a robust field of practice that has significant impact on faculty teaching practices. The Tracer study is in line with these practices, and extends them as they are revealed by associations such as the Professional and Organizational Development Network in Higher Education (POD), the community that has evolved from the Carnegie Foundation's promotion of SoTL, and the disciplinary communities focused on science, technology, engineering, and mathematics (STEM) higher education. Many of these efforts have demonstrated that teachers who participate in faculty development make changes in their practices. This is particularly the case when the development in which they participate engages faculty in change that is centered in their own disciplinary epistemologies, connects faculty to a community of practice, is data-driven, and becomes part of a faculty member's ongoing reflective teaching practice. (See, for example, the literature review in Henderson, Beach, and Finkelstein 2011 on promoting change in instructional practice in STEM.)

The Tracer Project grew out of such conditions and the desire to preserve and promulgate them. Like typical SoTL scholars, two of the principal investigators (Condon and Rutz) had long studied their own classroom teaching and their own students' learning. In thinking about such study on an institutional level, however, the research team recognized the need to study the faculty learning in faculty development, as well as students' learning in these faculty members' courses, and the need to address the larger institutional environments in which these levels of study take place. The spiral metaphor becomes more relevant and compelling as such investigations proceed. Individual faculty produce a shallow spiral when working alone and when employing only their own intuitions about improvement. SoTL has demonstrated over and over again the benefits that accrue when faculty use a research model on their own teaching (Hutchings, Huber, and Ciccone 2011). When they design instruments to gather data about their students' learning and then apply data-driven, empirical evidence to changes in pedagogy, the spiral lengthens, becomes taller. And when faculty engage in their own learning communities, the improved practices can spread more broadly throughout a college or university. Two of the programs studied by the Tracer Projects—the Critical Thinking Project at WSU and the Writing Across the Curriculum Project at Carleton—show this effect. A collective focus on improving how and what students learn provides a powerful motive for developing a faculty community of practice.

Intentional, Self-Directed Improvements in Teaching

The second site for faculty learning occurs in intentional, self-directed efforts on the part of faculty. Since at least 1990, when Carnegie Foundation president Ernest Boyer identified the need for a scholarship of teaching and learning, an impressive literature on SoTL has arisen. Even before that date, many researchers were already deeply engaged in that pursuit, though Boyer provided a focus for those efforts, and Carnegie Foundation backing surely helped with the argument that research in teaching and learning should count as research in any discipline.[1] Thus, the kind of serious intellectual work that is considered a legitimate use of research faculty time—whether in formal research or in experimentation with teaching—expanded considerably as a result of the SoTL movement and of course provided the center for SoTL as a field of inquiry. Consequently, the movement gained stature and, in the political sense, cover. However, one cannot overlook tensions within the SoTL community as to whether and when the work should be thought of as teaching, thus raising the bar for what is considered as professionally outstanding practice in teaching or as research, thus widening the definition of research in most disciplines (Hutchings, Huber, and Ciccone 2011). In addition to the more formal SoTL processes, faculty often make individual, intentional efforts at continually improving their teaching. Beyer, Taylor, and Gillmore (2013) mounted a broad study of faculty behaviors, demonstrating that even at a large research university, faculty spend more time on teaching than on research (and cf. Eagan et al. 2014). This second site for faculty learning has received a great deal of attention and produced solid research outcomes demonstrating that faculty can and do carry out their intentions to improve teaching. Even so, the research has yet to counter the commonly held assumption that faculty either don't care about teaching or that they care far less about it than they do about their research—which, according to the commonplace, deals with matters other than teaching.

Routine Faculty Development

The third site for faculty learning occurs during routine processes that are ubiquitous across institutions but that are not intended as sites for faculty learning or as events that promote better teaching. Yet these processes provide occasions for faculty to make important and actionable inferences about their own teaching and/or to provide feedback to colleagues to spur improvements in their teaching. To date, no research exists that establishes the connection between, say, a department's process of negotiating learning outcomes for its majors and an individual faculty member's changes in her course outcomes or teaching methods. Many guides exist on how to conduct classroom observations or how to evaluate faculty performance more generally. No study documents the effects of such activities on teaching performance. Summative evaluations of teaching performance—a critical aspect of high-stakes decisions about hiring, retention, and tenure and promotion—occur for every faculty member, and some occur every year. Yet no study of these summative evaluations attempts to conceive of them as an opportunity for faculty learning—faculty development—or to connect them to actual changes in teaching. Finally, higher education faculty live in an atmosphere that provides many occasions for learning about teaching. Department committee service focuses on curriculum to a greater or lesser extent; hallway conversations often involve talking about "what works" in the classroom. Engaging in departmental self-studies and ensuing external reviews exposes faculty to formative and summative judgments about teaching and learning in their departments or programs. These sites for learning, to date, provide routine, non-programmed learning. While they are not intended as faculty development in the direct and intentional ways of the first two sites, this third site has great potential, as the current project revealed, to join into a generative culture of teaching and learning and to produce significant faculty learning about teaching. And that learning can also be connected to changes in teaching that produce changes in student learning. Institutions that have achieved such an extensive generative culture of teaching and learning are perhaps in the best position to counter the prevailing assumptions about faculty and teaching; however, ironically, these institutions may feel less compelled to address that assumption, since it is so clearly not true on their campuses.

Connecting Faculty Learning with Student Learning

The Tracer Project studied two very different campuses to evaluate the pathway from professional development to student learning. These campuses have produced widespread, concerted, and continuous faculty efforts to reflect on and improve their teaching, along with methods for establishing whether the changes that faculty have made as a result of that study actually do improve students' learning. In the process of investigating formal faculty development, perspectives emerge about how to make the outcomes of other kinds of intentional faculty development—SoTL research, as well as more informal and individual efforts—more visible, by moving them out of faculty members' solitary offices or, in some cases, specialized or niche conferences and publications, and into a larger campus community that can make common cause around improving teaching and learning. If higher education is to demonstrate its effectiveness in these areas, it first needs to overcome the commonplace that asserts its ineffectiveness. The visibility of research efforts to audiences within and beyond the academy is critical to this first step.

While, unfortunately, faculty who fit the stereotype do exist, most college faculty actually want to—and do—work on their teaching competencies. The research of Beyer, Taylor, and Gillmore (2013) at the University of Washington reveals that faculty almost universally feel the need to work on their teaching and seek out ways to do so. Their study presents a data-driven rebuttal of the commonplace notion that faculty care about their research but not their teaching. Instead, faculty devote significant amounts of time to examining and improving their teaching practices—above and beyond the time they spend in activities directly related to teaching (such as preparing for and attending class, grading papers, and meeting with students).

However, as the interviews and surveys of Beyer, Taylor, and Gillmore (2013) reveal, faculty often do this work in isolation, hoping to build better practices by examining what they see as their successes and failures and then making changes based on teaching experience. Others proceed by word of mouth or by lore, adopting practices that their colleagues believe have been successful in their classrooms. Still others attend formal development opportunities, though this number is lower than the numbers in the first two categories; colleges and universities provide limited funding for faculty development, so scheduling conflicts and limitations on the number of people such events accommodate means that relatively few faculty can attend those formal events. Professional societies in all disciplines provide additional opportunities, including both face-to-face and virtual events. For example, a plethora of virtual events have been made available through organizations such as the Association for American Colleges and Universities (AAC&U) and annual conferences provide sessions about teaching and learning in their various disciplines. Clearly, college teachers work on their teaching. Their progress may be slow, but the important point here is that faculty see the need to work on their teaching and take steps to do so, using one or more of the types of learning laid out above. Organized faculty development can make a difference in faculty practice, and, as the Tracer Project has found, this almost universal motivation to improve teaching opens the possibilities for developing a productive culture of teaching and learning. Faculty welcome such development, increasing the likelihood that it will result in positive changes in faculty teaching practices.

The Tracer results amplify this general finding with evidence that confirms the extent to which faculty seek out and value development opportunities. Moreover, findings show the extent to which an institution can support a community or a culture of teaching and learning by taking note of formal offerings as well as informal or routine development opportunities that generate powerful leverage on faculty members' desire for improvement. When an institution invites faculty to make common cause of improving teaching, then faculty development of all kinds comes out into the open. Tying improvements in teaching to improvements in students' learning provides evidence that the improvements are working, and thus provides motivation—and data— to continue improving teaching.

This is the challenge the Tracer Project undertook: the effects of changes in faculty practice in higher education need to be measured in terms of changes in students' learning. Much of the research on faculty development in higher education has tended to evaluate participants' experiences and their self-reported changes in teaching, stopping short of the ways that faculty bring their new knowledge into their courses (see Brooks et al. 2011; Chism and Szabó 1997). End-of-workshop surveys may laud a workshop or program, but formal follow-up on the ways participants adapt, apply, and assess what they have learned is seldom documented. Those studies investigating impact on teaching have rested heavily on faculty self-reported data (e.g. Macdonald et al. 2004; Dancy and Henderson 2010; Fullan 2001; Garet et al. 2001).

At the University of Minnesota (Brooks, Marsh, Wilcox, and Cohen 2011), researchers specifically sought more "robust and reliable measures" than faculty satisfaction with the professional development experiences for evaluating the effects of faculty development on student learning. However, the researchers' only method for detecting effects in student learning was to administer a closed-ended survey to faculty participants about their perceptions of their students' learning, thus stopping short of any direct study of student learning outcomes. Studies that make direct observations of changes in teaching proactive are less common in higher education. Ebert-May et al. (2011) have directly observed faculty and compared self-reported changes in practice that suggest faculty overreport change. Even rarer are studies that extend to student learning. Bernstein, Johnson, and Smith (2000) used student surveys to determine that there were no significant benefits to students' learning based on faculty members' participation in professional development at the University of Nebraska. Nonetheless, this finding may, in part, be limited in its explanatory value since researchers collected only surveys from students self-reporting changes in learning.

While studies on the impact of faculty development seldom extend to student learning, there is extensive research on the broad relationship between specific teaching practices and student learning. Indeed, this is the focus of traditional SoTL investigations in which faculty explore the relationship between teaching and learning in their own classrooms. Substantial work within the STEM disciplines, in educational psychology, and in studies of teaching and learning more generally provides robust evidence of the importance of student-centered, active learning practices on what students learn (Bransford, Brown, and Cocking 2000; Hake 1998; Johnson, Johnson, and Holubec 1998; Singer, Nielsen, and Schweingruber 2012). Richard Light offers substantial—though again, self-reported—evidence that establishes a direct relationship between the amounts of writing assigned in a course and the students' engagement in the course (Light 2001).

In addition, numerous scholars in STEM disciplines have documented student learning gains in relation to specific pedagogies such as interactive, small group collaborations as well as undergraduate research (Ebert-May, Batlzi, and Weber 2006; Hoellwarth, Moelter, and Knight 2005; Laursen et al. 2010; Middlecamp 2008; Freeman et al.

2014). However, the need continues for direct links between professional development experiences, changes in practice, and specific gains in student learning. Moreover, educational research in STEM tends to arise within a specific STEM discipline. Few studies of teaching or student learning bridge higher education communities (Henderson, Beach, and Finkelstein 2011). Such studies across STEM disciplines focus on the relationship between active teaching techniques and a narrow student achievement outcome or failure rate (Freeman et al. 2014) but fail to identify the professional learning that led to active teaching.

As the data emerge to support widespread connections between faculty learning and student learning, another fact emerges: on campuses where multiple faculty development efforts coalesce, productive cultures of teaching and learning may be identified. Such cultures may form in the presence of certain conditions, which the Tracer Project identifies. Briefly, these conditions include the presence of multiple initiatives and their visibility on campus; the incorporation of attention to teaching and learning in the expectations for faculty in hiring, orientation, and reward systems; the aspects of faculty development that encourage shared efforts across disciplines to improve teaching and learning; and extended, common-cause efforts around a specific learning outcome (e.g., evaluating writing portfolios). While this list is hardly comprehensive, all these factors contribute to creating out of individual efforts an effective culture of teaching and learning. These aspects may manifest in various ways on a given campus, so this study provides an initial list of indicators to help identify the signs of an emergent culture and to actively nurture that culture.

This culture is of particular interest to those concerned that changes in teaching practice engendered by professional development experiences may be short-lived. Huber and Hutchings (2005) argue that a national teaching commons for the ongoing exchange of information is foundational to enhancements in teaching and learning across the country. Data from the Tracer Project support the positive effects of a community that engages collectively and individually in a continuous cycle of learning and improvement focused on teaching and learning, much as advocated by Huber. This learning community knits together the opportunities and experiences of all its members into a fabric that supports ongoing change and long-term impact. Similarly, this culture integrates improvements in teaching across the institution—spiraling outward to promote opportunities for faculty to improve practices that address long-term, higher-order student learning fundamental to critical thinking, knowledge making, or effective argumentation.

This book offers additional research on three areas encompassed by SoTL and POD: that faculty development influences teaching practices; that teaching improved through faculty development can be documented; and that students benefit from innovative teaching techniques as shown by improved learning outcomes. Tracer research confirms or amplifies those conclusions. In addition, the study identifies the effects of faculty development on students' learning, as well as on building a productive and effective culture of teaching and learning on a campus. Such a culture helps establish a more collaborative process of improving teaching and learning, as well as bringing existing efforts into more public forums, where their visibility itself helps counter the widely shared belief that faculty do not care about teaching.

In response to burgeoning, yet generalized, critiques of U.S. higher education today (again, see Arum and Roksa 2010; Delbanco 2012; Keeling and Hersh 2012), faculty need to understand what does, and does not, support student learning within particular institutional contexts as well as on the larger scale. The scholarship of teaching and learning provides one kind of antidote, in its attention to beliefs and practices in the classroom as well as at the departmental and institutional levels. Here, the reference is to a broadly defined SoTL, in which scholar-practitioners share ideas and research on their teaching with others outside, as well as inside, their colleges and universities (Huber and Hutchings 2005; Hutchings et al. 2011). SoTL research not only contributes to and builds upon knowledge about teaching and learning, but also points to practical ways of improving teaching and learning (see Hubball and Clarke 2010 and Weimer 2006). If changes are broad and long term, rather than confined within a given course, then examinations of change must take place on the institutional scale, as a collaborative exploration among faculty.

The Tracer Project also responds to great demands on higher education to improve teaching and learning, especially in light of changing student demographics, emerging technologies, and the continual reexamination of the goals and desired outcomes of higher education. The good news so far is the rise of new pedagogies and new approaches to teaching (including SoTL), a higher profile for faculty development, and an emphasis on improving teaching both in pre-service teachers (graduate students) and in-service faculty. The bad news is that the pathway between faculty development and changing practice is unclear, and many throw up their hands in surrender over seeking links to learning. What's more, few look outward to the effects of attending to these connections on institutional culture. Fortunately, between SoTL and POD (overlapping communities, to be sure), one gains insights about how to begin—or, perhaps, how to set some parameters.

Organization of the Book

This book is organized into seven chapters, divided into three sections. The first section, chapters 1–3, sets the research stage, describes the contexts for the study, describes the theory of change, and includes descriptions of the mixed methods employed throughout the study. The research findings are explained in chapters 4–6, where the focus moves from effects on individual faculty to the spread of effects beyond specific faculty learning events to the effects of faculty learning on student learning. Finally, chapter 7 offers reflections on support for teaching and learning in higher education, including recommendations for further research.

Summary

With faculty development as the point of departure, the Tracer Project contributes to knowledge about practices in teaching and learning. In pragmatic terms, this book describes productive teaching practices, ways of evaluating faculty development, teaching, and learning, and institutional environments that support these practices and attitudes. In the absence of evidence for, or against, faculty development effects on teaching and learning, institutions can hardly justify spending money on it. How will institutions draw participants into faculty development without such evidence? How will institutions know that their teachers are becoming better teachers? When studying student learning in an institution of higher education, how can anyone ignore an analysis of how faculty members develop their own methods and processes for learning about teaching? And what happens at the institutional level when faculty development programming becomes ubiquitous, curricular, and a part of faculty members' daily lives? How can the effects of this programming be known, and how can they be studied at different kinds of institutions?

This book offers higher education a place to begin posing and addressing these difficult questions. As is the case with a great deal of research, difficulties began with articulating the questions in ways that would bear on all the players: faculty, students, administrators, and the institution—as an active entity. Some may doubt that a small college and a large research university can find common ground as well as exploit significant differences to get at important principles for successful teaching and learning practices for students—as experienced and modeled by their classroom faculty. The Tracer Project shows that disparate institutions can collaborate and learn from one another in this domain. If institutions as different as Carleton College and Washington State University can succeed in such an effort, other institutions may well benefit from this example.

2 Sites of Faculty Learning

Faculty learning about teaching inevitably reflects the institutional characteristics and opportunities/sites for learning that are available to faculty at a given institution. In any particular context, faculty learning takes place constantly, through multiple means and within varied locations—whether spatial or institutional.

Evaluating the effects of faculty development on teaching and learning is similarly complicated by the necessity to consider each study and its results in terms of its institutional context. The vast differences in those contexts—greatly varying sizes, demographics, governance, and curricula—provide one of the strengths of the Tracer Project. Research findings from such different settings are more likely to provide a useful model for generating and evaluating faculty development programs at any institution of higher education. Even so, this project provides more of a range of possibilities and actions that might be adapted for differing contexts than it does a model; in fact, this research reinforces longtime SoTL scholar Peter Felten's (2013) statement that good research on teaching and learning must be contextualized within the particular institutional environments in which it is conducted (222–223).

This chapter, then, sets the context for research at the two institutions, providing a high-level view of the teaching and learning environments (including demographics, institutional missions, and structural support) at each institution and a more granular view of faculty development experiences (including faculty participation and motivations to participate) at each. This study draws on data from a large land grant university and a small liberal arts college. Institutional differences inevitably affect approaches to faculty development and faculty tendencies to participate, though common teaching and learning initiatives blunt the impact of such differences, in substance if not in approach. Despite obvious differences in size, location, and mission, the two institutions feature similar structures for faculty development as well as some important variations. Both institutions have long-standing programs for Writing Across the

Curriculum (WAC) that include specific workshops as well as portfolio assessment of student writing conducted by faculty readers. WAC workshops emphasize writing as a pedagogy, a practical means of learning by doing. Portfolio assessment at both campuses occurs at mid-career for the students and offers faculty the opportunity to read student work from all disciplines in a setting that fosters dialogue about writing in general and the ways that writing can be taught.

In addition to the WAC emphasis, each campus has specialized faculty development programs unique to their institutional contexts. The study targeted faculty portfolio raters on both campuses, as well as faculty who participated in WAC and/or Critical Thinking at WSU, and WAC and/or Quantitative Inquiry, Reasoning, and Knowledge (QuIRK) at Carleton College. Data collection at WSU focused on the persistence of faculty learning about Critical Thinking after an active faculty development program had expired. Data collection at Carleton was more contemporary, as the QuIRK program for faculty was ongoing at the time of the study.

Carleton College and WSU Institutional and Demographic Teaching/Learning Environments

Carleton characterizes itself as highly oriented toward teaching and learning, providing "a true liberal arts education, a curriculum that challenges our students to learn broadly and think deeply." Faculty, according to Carleton's public claims, are "highly respected scholars, researchers, and practitioners in their own field. But above all, their first priority is teaching." The college has a small number of students (roughly 2,000) and offers a Bachelor of Arts degree in thirty-nine majors. It has small average class sizes (eighteen students; 61 percent of classes have fewer than twenty students), small faculty to undergraduate ratios (1:9), few temporary or non-tenure track faculty (37 part-time faculty of 226 total), promotion and evaluation procedures that heavily weigh teaching and student evaluations in addition to research, and regular and frequent faculty development activities (weekly, yearly, and ad-hoc activities).

WSU self-description and branding processes ("World-Class, Face-to-Face") include teaching excellence, but research takes center stage: "One of the nation's top public research institutions, WSU stands among 96 U.S. public and private universities with very high research activity, according to The Carnegie Foundation classification. *U.S. News and World Report* consistently ranks the University among the top 60 public universities. Many academic programs win recognition for excellence" (WSU self-study for reaccreditation). The university, which has its main campus in Pullman and branch campuses in Vancouver, Tri-Cities, and Spokane, enrolls roughly 25,000 total students (23,000 undergraduate and 2,000 graduate students, 13 percent of whom are part-time students). The university offers 200 fields of study across eleven colleges. Almost 40 percent of its classes enroll fewer than twenty students, and the faculty-to-undergraduate ratio is 1 to 16. WSU depends heavily upon non-tenure track faculty at all levels, though most extensively for lower division undergraduate courses. WSU employs the Full-Time Equivalent (FTE) of 230 temporary faculty (full-time, non-tenure-track; plus part-time) of a total 1,200 instructional faculty, in addition to 900 part-time graduate teaching assistants (Provost's Fact Book, 2012). Like many large state-assisted universities, WSU has moved, *de facto*, toward a two-tiered faculty. Thus, most of the temporary faculty are full-time, long-time teachers with rich experience and initial qualifications that closely parallel faculty on the tenure track (i.e., PhDs, publications, strong teaching experience). Many of these non-tenured/temporary faculty have taught at the school for more than seven years—as long as someone who has earned tenure—and are considered to be excellent teachers. Quite a few maintain active research agendas, despite the fact that their appointments are dedicated to teaching. For tenure-track faculty, promotion procedures are equally weighted between research and teaching, with less weight on service (the most common weighting is 40 percent research, 40 percent teaching, and 20 percent service, a typical distribution at research universities). This distribution is reinforced in both annual reviews and in promotion and tenure decisions.

In addition to differences in size and mission, WSU and Carleton diverge in relation to student body composition, as shown in table 2.1. WSU students range across a wider spectrum of ages, are somewhat more racially and culturally diverse than Carleton students, live off campus more than Carleton students, and can attend college part-time, unlike Carleton students. Carleton is also much more academically selective in freshmen admissions than the larger, public WSU.

Differences in mission, faculty development, and demographics produced differences in the study at the two schools. For example, collecting or using quantitative data was more difficult because of Carleton's much smaller student body (small *n*s affected Carleton's rubric analyses of student writing samples), and robust qualitative data (in the form of interviews and observations) were harder to collect at WSU. In both cases, the teams adapted (rather than adopted) each other's methodologies, demonstrating the point of studying two such different institutions together: rather than developing a "one size fits all" model, this study illustrates how even very different institutions can use each other's approaches to produce, if not identical sets of data, at least comparable ones.

Faculty Development at Carleton and WSU

Despite these demographic and institutional differences, researchers collected enough qualitative and quantitative data to demonstrate that faculty at both institutions were interested in student learning. In part, this conclusion stems from the effort to locate a comparison group of faculty who had not participated in formal faculty development activities. At WSU, researchers secured a list of all faculty and deleted from that list the names of faculty who had attended formal development events offered by the Campus Writing Programs, the General Education Program, or the Center for Teaching, Learning, and Technology. This reduced the list of 1,237 instructional faculty to 844.

TABLE 2.1. DEMOGRAPHIC COMPARISON OF STUDENTS AT WASHINGTON STATE UNIVERSITY AND CARLETON COLLEGE

	WSU	CARLETON
Student population over age 25	19%	0%
Non-U.S. citizens	4% (2011)	9.8% (2011)
Non-white (self-identified)	26%	22.2%
Live off-campus	0% of first-year students; nearly 100% of all others	10%
Part-time	13%	0% (2012)
Transfer students	64%	less than 1% (2012)
Acceptance rate	70%	26% (2010)
SAT critical reading scores of accepted students	460 (25% scored at or below and 570 (25% scored above)	670 (25% scored at or below) and 760 (25% scored at or above)
SAT math	470 (25% scored at or below) and 600 (25% scored above)	670 (25% scored at or below) and 760 (25% scored at or above)
SAT writing	450 (25% scored at or below) and 550 (25% scored above)	660 (25% scored at or below) and 750 (25% scored at or above)
ACT composition	20 (25% scored at or below) and 25 (25% scored above)	29 (25% scored at or below) and 33 (25% scored at or above)

Note: 2013 is the default year for these statistics unless otherwise noted.

Half that list (422) were sent a brief survey asking what faculty development opportunities they had attended. The survey yielded 148 responses (a rate of 35 percent), only three of which were from faculty who testified that they had attended no such events. While it is likely that non-attenders are hidden among the non-responders, the proportion of responders who attended events resulted in formulating a group of "low-participating faculty" in place of a traditional control group, since locating a sufficient number of *non*-participators was impractical, if not impossible.

Carleton researchers ran up against similar problems in identifying a comparison group of non-participators after comparing the list of all faculty teaching on campus (234 total faculty in the 2010–2011 academic year) to the proliferation of faculty development participation lists (including ten years of WAC workshops and writing portfolio rating sessions, three years of quantitative reasoning workshops, three years of winter break workshop lists, and five years of Carleton's Learning and Teaching Center lunches and book groups). Whenever individuals were identified as potential non-participators, soon they would be found on a new participation list, attending a lunch talk, or having moved on from Carleton. The original list of 100 potential non-participators (in writing and quantitative reasoning activities) eventually shrank to fewer than 30 individuals. To identify a larger pool of potential research participants, Tracer researchers sought faculty at the extreme ends of participation—more and less active.

On both campuses, faculty participated in both formal and routine forms of faculty development in their daily professional lives, garnering teaching inspiration from their peers as well as experts. Researchers defined faculty development operationally, as any activity that provides faculty and staff with new ideas for teaching (approaches, content, technology, and /or methodologies for assessing learning) or with tools to analyze and improve their current methods. Such opportunities for faculty development are grounded in the premise that faculty learning is a sociocultural activity informed and actualized by everyday interaction with colleagues (Webster-Wright 2009; Putnam and Borko 2000). Formal opportunities for faculty development are activities described by program leaders and advertised as helping faculty learn how to become better teachers. Routine forms of faculty development may be activities that faculty engage in ostensibly for other purposes (such as faculty promotion evaluations, student learning assessment, departmental reviews, institutional reviews, or campus planning committees), but that also help faculty reflect on and study, in perhaps limited ways, teaching and learning in their own classrooms or on their campuses.

Formal and Self-Directed Faculty Development at Carleton College

From 2009 to 2011, Carleton faculty participated in both of these forms of faculty development in relatively high numbers. In the 2010–2011 Higher Education Research Institute survey of faculty at Carleton and many more institutions across the nation (Hurtado et al. 2012), 76.8 percent of the Carleton faculty respondents reported that they had participated in a "teaching enhancement workshop."[1] Such workshops included the following:

- a yearly array of voluntary activities in the first weeks of winter break ("Winter Workshops")
- Perlman Center for Learning and Teaching (locally known as the Learning and Teaching Center, or LTC) weekly lunchtime talks, book groups, teaching circles, a student observer program, and consultations
- an all-faculty retreat before the start of each academic year
- new faculty orientation before the start of each academic year and a more intensive workshop on teaching and learning in the winter break
- curricular initiatives, generally funded externally, which also often feature faculty development opportunities
- ad hoc activities proposed and organized by faculty or staff

Carleton uses an organic method for planning and executing formal faculty development. Faculty and staff members design the programming based on their own and their colleagues' interests (with college and outside grant funding). Administrators rarely introduce a workshop topic on their own without faculty and staff support. Faculty and staff participants—who span the curriculum and levels of seniority—learn about a wide range of topics related to teaching and learning. In form, the faculty and staff leaders of these faculty development activities often employ the same sorts of teaching strategies that they use in their Carleton classrooms; activities include time for discussion and opportunities for active or experiential learning and self-reflection. The following short observation of a December workshop is typical of Carleton faculty development in its leadership, activities, and even some content:

> The visiting organizer (John Bean, of Seattle University, a well-known scholar in Writing Across the Curriculum [WAC] and returning visitor to Carleton) began the three-day workshop by describing how the general principle behind teaching academic writing in the disciplines is to start by thinking about the problems that students need to wrestle with in their classes (and this could be dozens of problems). He illustrated this point by describing how he gave the students in his courses a class problem ahead of time and, instead of telling the class to "read chapter eight" for homework, asked them to come back the next day ready to discuss this problem with material and/or ideas from the readings. The organizer then advised the group of twenty-two Carleton faculty and staff that these course problems were best if they were "messy, ill-structured" or "intriguing." He ended this part of the workshop by opening the topic up for discussion.
>
> In the conversations that followed, staff, faculty, and the workshop organizers (a resident expert on the topic was co-leader of the workshop) reflected on both theoretical understandings of how students learn and the specificities of teaching at Carleton. In the next part of the workshop, the leaders transferred these discussions into smaller group work on individuals' assignment-design projects.

Participants left this particular workshop having learned how to design writing assignments that

- aligned with course learning goals, including a description of how to use a "backward design" approach to create a new course and assignments
- included quantitative data and quantitative reasoning
- included tasks and support needed for students at different developmental stages or with different writing and learning experiences
- encouraged students to pay attention to audience and helped them learn how to write within and beyond the disciplines
- provided faculty members with a good head start in developing an assignment for a future class

Such a combination of discussion, research-based pedagogical instruction, and experiential learning characterizes Carleton's faculty development. Over the last fifteen years, faculty and staff members have also repeatedly returned to the topics of writing, quantitative reasoning, visual literacy, and assignment design. This curricular approach to faculty development helps older faculty members continue to develop their teaching of these topics while beginning to enculturate newer faculty into positive approaches and practices.

Looking more specifically at the formal opportunities aligned with writing and quantitative reasoning, the focus of this study, Carleton's faculty development curriculum typically inspires a move from teaching faculty new concepts or techniques, using multiple exposures, to faculty adaptation or innovation of teaching materials. For example, multiple workshops and summer course development grants have supported faculty in activating concepts common to writing and quantitative reasoning. In both cases, faculty are asked to

- articulate course learning goals
- scaffold assignments in the course by staging assignments to build up to larger assignments and assigning drafts as part of the assignment
- help students pay attention to audience in writing and oral reports
- develop a rubric for evaluating student work
- encourage students to write multiple drafts and revise in response to feedback
- provide students with clear, helpful, and timely comments on their work
- provide students with exemplars
- incorporate peer review
- encourage help-seeking habits for all students (writing center, library, professors, staff, and peers)

For quantitative reasoning, specifically, faculty are prompted to

- institute a quantitative habit of mind for students
- help students implement quantitative methods correctly
- help students interpret and evaluate quantitative information thoughtfully
- help students communicate effectively with quantitative data
- give students ill-structured problems and assignments that involve real-world problems
- help students visually represent numbers to support their arguments

For WAC, specifically, faculty

- analyze assignments for effectiveness
- make comments effective—focus on the larger/global issues in earlier drafts and then comment on the grammatical or other small errors in later versions

- teach students to write clear prose
- teach students to write with clear organization
- teach students to use appropriate diction
- teach students to use Standard English effectively
- teach students to understand writing as a process
- teach students how to apply forms of attribution and citation as appropriate
- teach students about academic honesty
- help students develop confidence in their writing
- help students to become self-aware and self-reflective writers
- help students develop their information literacy (research skills, citation, and documentation)

As Tracer researchers look for the impact of formal faculty development at Carleton, these themes are expected to be reflected in faculty descriptions of their new knowledge and in the changes that they make in their teaching.

Formal and Self-Directed Faculty Development at WSU

An institution as large as WSU often has a centralized center for teaching and learning where faculty know they can seek out support for their teaching. Such a center typically offers generic programming about developing learning objectives, writing syllabi, designing effective course assignments, teaching with new technologies, and so forth. Often, the center conducts or collaborates with faculty on research centered in specific teaching innovations. During the period covered by the current research, WSU ran the Center for Teaching, Learning, and Technology (CTLT), which served all of the above functions, in addition to maintaining the campus's online learning environment (often called a classroom management system, or CMS) and training faculty in best practices in online and hybrid teaching. That unit was first absorbed into a recently created University College and then gradually dismantled to provide funding to establish the new college. Its remaining vestige is a two-person unit called the Office of Assessment and Innovation, which offers a very narrow range of support, primarily aimed at helping departments with annual reports and program evaluations.

Unlike Carleton, then, WSU, at the time of this writing, offers no centralized faculty development, other than an annual New Faculty Orientation and an annual WAC workshop offered by the Campus Writing Programs. Previously, however, CTLT was an active and effective partner in, for example, redesigning Economics 101 into an online course; reforming the School of Veterinary Medicine's clinical curriculum, including tools for assessing its effectiveness; programming several innovative online learning environments and participating in the national conversations about online teaching and learning; and, most appropriate to this study, serving as one of three partner programs in WSU's Critical Thinking Project. That project forms one of the three areas studied in the Tracer Project, along with two functions of the Campus Writing Programs: annual WAC workshops and ongoing rating sessions for the Junior Writing Portfolio.

The lack of centralized support for faculty development results in a wide range of activities developed in the eleven colleges or in the sixty departments. Thus an overall description of faculty development at WSU, like the one above for Carleton, is impossible. There is no mechanism for cataloging all that is going on, nor can one conclusively determine the depth of participation in formal opportunities at WSU. Tracer researchers obtained some insight by understanding the formal opportunities that past participants in the Critical Thinking Project have exploited. Even after the university abolished the CTLT, most (74 percent) of 168 faculty research participants had attended at least one formal faculty development event per year, and more than half (55 percent) reported attending three or more such events per year. These figures include 56 faculty employed part- or full-time as temporary faculty, many of whom revealed that they attend all the workshops they can find, since their positions are vulnerable and continued employment hinges totally on the department or program's needs and on their effectiveness as teachers. Many of this group also taught in programs that sponsored multiple faculty development events, so they reported attending more than ten such events per semester—more than twenty per year. Thus it is clear that there are in fact rich opportunities at least in some departments and that most faculty are capitalizing on them.

Most departments hold pre-semester retreats, where at least some attention is paid to improving teaching in the department. However, the majority of formal "teaching enhancement" faculty development venues were elective at both institutions; chairs of departments, program leaders, and friends/colleagues may have encouraged individual faculty to participate in them, but no one was required to attend or overtly censured for turning down one of these opportunities. In addition, these programs and activities were led by faculty and staff and not solely by administrators. Thus, the popularity of these workshops and rating sessions (and leadership roles that faculty take in them) was another signifier of individual faculty and staff members' concern and interest in teaching issues.

For current purposes, data on faculty development at WSU describe the three initiatives listed above: a follow-up with faculty who engaged with the Critical Thinking Project (1999–2003), faculty participants in WAC workshops, and faculty raters for the Junior Writing Portfolio.

The necessity to focus on only a few development avenues highlights a major difference in these two types of institution. At Carleton, faculty development operates more as a single entity, where even if the initiative, like the one associated with quantitative reasoning, is run by a small group, its offerings invite the whole community. By contrast, a large state university operates more on a piecemeal basis, where even a very large, campus-wide initiative like the Critical Thinking Project can only reach about

330 faculty—a number larger than Carleton's entire faculty, but still only one-sixth of WSU's teaching cadre (the total of tenure track faculty, temporary faculty, and graduate student teachers).

From one place to another, faculty development stemming from routine events and processes probably looks more the same than more formal or intentional forms can. From the smallest to the largest institutions, departments set requirements for concentrations, design curricula to allow students to meet those requirements in a sensible and timely way, and perform some sort of evaluation to ensure that the plans are being carried out and that the student experience is beneficial. Committee service is ubiquitous, as is some form of faculty governance, whether at the department, college, or university level (or all levels). Thus, opportunities for faculty development from these processes at a large institution such as WSU are more congruent with those at a smaller institution such as Carleton than are the systematic opportunities for formal faculty development. Scale may differ—and with it the precise location of an activity—but the activities themselves are quite similar.

At Carleton, all tenure-track faculty learn about teaching by participating in institutionally required activities such as promotion reviews, departmental reviews, faculty meetings, curricular reviews, institutional assessments (for accreditation), and campus studies (every ten years and/or as initiated by new college presidents), third-year reviews and tenure reviews (although senior faculty do not always have to serve on review committees) that include multiple observations of faculty teaching, discussions about teaching and learning, and study of extensive student evaluations of teaching practices. Departments and the larger college participated in assessment efforts for the purpose of college accreditation and general accountability (although individuals participate more or less based on their leadership roles and their interest), which also included study of student learning artifacts (e. g., senior theses). At Carleton, some of the most institutionally influential changes in faculty experiences of development activities and approaches to teaching have been initiated by accreditation reviews and campus studies, which identified areas for curricular—as well as structural—development. Even Carleton's "town hall" form of faculty governance exposes the general faculty to new initiatives, details of progress from existing initiatives, and opportunities to join initiatives still in the ideational or planning stages. These routine, teaching-focused initiatives or occasions, this study has observed, are a source for faculty development—especially difficult to quantify and observe—that happens in formal processes, as well as ad-hoc meetings between faculty members in hallways, outside of classrooms, over lunch, and via email. At Carleton, faculty who were less active in formal faculty development could still be heard discussing pedagogy and student learning in ways that reflected ongoing conversations in formal and intentional forms of faculty development on campus (e. g., in relation to writing and quantitative reasoning).

Similarly, WSU faculty identify a number of places where they "pick up pointers" about teaching, even though the event does not purposely address improving one's teaching. For example, service on departmental curriculum committees exposes committee members to the plan behind major concentrations, and course proposals developed by colleagues provide insight into new or different ways of addressing the curriculum, a variety of assignment types, a range of teaching methods and grading philosophies, and so on. Participating on whatever level in a departmental self-study—for accreditation or for external review—provides everyone in the department with the opportunity to review their courses, think together about their curriculum design, and evaluate students' progress. Departmental colloquia engage faculty in each other's research interests and in teaching interests and practices as well, prompting attendees to consider adapting a colleague's assignments and approaches to attendees' own courses. Reviewing junior colleagues' files for tenure and promotion or acting as a mentor for a junior colleague provide intensive looks at one colleague's successes (or failures) and at the course syllabi and assignments responsible for whatever degree of success the colleague has experienced. Faculty cite all these service activities and more as they trace the influences on their own teaching.

For WSU faculty who do not participate extensively in formal professional development, these routine opportunities may act as the only source—aside from hallway conversations and their own independent reading—for new ideas about teaching and learning. At an institution like WSU, developing the kinds of campus-wide faculty development opportunities present at Carleton is difficult, if not impossible; hence, considering how to make the most of routine development becomes extremely important.

Assessing Writing Portfolios

At both Carleton and WSU, assessing or rating student writing portfolios provides an intensive opportunity to learn about teaching for large numbers of faculty. This activity is routine in that it is required for operation of the general education requirements at both campuses. However, by virtue of its design—faculty must read and discuss a large volume of student work in the context of the assignments that prompt it—it has the potential to serve as a potent form of formal faculty development. At Carleton, where portfolio rating was modeled on the WSU activity, it was specifically designed to serve this dual purpose. At WSU, the formal faculty development component emerged from the necessity of the routine event. Table 2.2 shows the scale of the activity at the two institutions.

At WSU, approximately 4,500 portfolios are rated each year, by an active group of about 50 raters. In any given year, approximately 350 faculty on campus have been trained at one time or another as raters. Faculty who have signed off on a student's work for the portfolio (approximately 1,200 each year) or who have taught a Writing in the Major course (approximately 400 per year) are invited to become raters. Those who come forward are trained as Tier I raters (rating the two timed writings that are part of WSU's portfolio); then, if they do well, they are invited to train for Tier II, where raters

TABLE 2.2. COMPARATIVE DATA ON PORTFOLIO RATING AT
WASHINGTON STATE UNIVERSITY AND CARLETON COLLEGE

	WSU	CARLETON
Number of portfolios per academic year	4500	450
Number of faculty raters trained	350	140
Number required for one year's ratings	Approximately 50	35
Rating sessions held	Approximately 50, as needed throughout the year	1, in June
Percentage of raters from departments other than English	82	88

look at whole portfolios. Because of the sheer number of portfolios, the process is very much a mass production enterprise. Each session begins with a norming exercise, and raters who are having a difficult time with a given sample are encouraged to consult with each other about the writing. Raters are paid on an hourly basis ($20/hour for Tier I; $40/hour at Tier II). During norming, during consultation, and after each session, raters carry on a lively conversation about the portfolios they are reading.

At Carleton, where approximately 450 portfolios are collected each year, ratings occur during three days in June, usually in the week following graduation. About 35 faculty raters gather on three consecutive mornings. They gather for a light breakfast, then a norming session, and then rating. As at WSU, they are encouraged to consult on any portfolios that might present difficulties and to read the attached assignment prompts. Each half-day session is followed by lunch and another session for faculty to negotiate final ratings for portfolios that they disagreed on (usually these are the portfolios that one faculty member rates very high or very low, but portfolios are also read twice if the rater is a staff member, as opposed to a faculty member). Raters are paid a flat fee of $360 for the three days of rating. As at WSU, conversations about the writing are lively and range widely. Because portfolio rating is considered a formal form of faculty development at Carleton, faculty and organizers come together at the end of the session to reflect on the rating process, on the students' writing, and on lessons learned about teaching and student learning at Carleton.

Sites of Faculty Learning

In both institutions, significant numbers of faculty demonstrate their interest in learning about teaching and learning by participating in formal, intentional faculty development experiences. At Carleton, this can be quantified as approximately three quarters of the faculty. At WSU, it is harder to quantify the reach of formal professional development because of its decentralized structure. However, at least 540 WSU faculty participated in the formal activities of the Critical Thinking Project and WAC during the study's interval.

The emergence of Carleton's large range of formal offerings over the past two decades demonstrates the effects of faculty-centered, carefully planned sets of activities combined with a shared governance system (Smith 1978) and sense of community that is formed around faculty development activities (Willett 2013). Tracer researchers see similar developments at other small liberal arts colleges, which may mean that such an environment makes establishing systematic faculty development easier. At the same time, enough small liberal arts colleges have difficulty mounting such efforts to demonstrate that while size matters, it is no guarantee of success. However, at a large, state-assisted, land grant university like WSU, scale acts as a strong constraint on faculty development—at least, on formal types of development. At smaller schools where faculty, staff, and students serve with administrators on governing committees, faculty can insist on opportunities and begin initiatives more easily; at a large university where the central administration is at best apathetic toward faculty development— and, as at WSU, even antagonistic toward it—issues of scale, of sheer numbers, force most formal faculty development down the food chain into colleges or departments. Thus, rather than creating one cross-campus culture of teaching and learning, cultures must arise separately, within different areas of the curriculum.

However, looking at our comparisons, one feature stands out. On each campus, these successful activities sprang from faculty values and interests. At WSU, the Critical Thinking Project helped faculty pursue their goals of promoting students' higher-order thinking skills. Addressing that priority allowed the team mounting the workshops and other activities to get faculty to take a serious look at their own teaching practices and to make substantial changes—a change process that continues into the present. While central administrative support for the project waned once the grant from the Fund for Improvement of Post-Secondary Education (FIPSE) ran out, colleges, departments, and programs kept the process alive within their own faculties. At Carleton, the particular student body demographics and the low student/faculty ratio meant that critical thinking in general did not present the kind of challenge that WSU faculty encountered. Still, quantitative reasoning did, as evidenced in students' work in their writing portfolios. Out of that faculty-articulated concern QuIRK developed, which has contributed significantly to faculty practices across Carleton's curriculum. Finally, the comparisons between the two institutions' portfolio systems as faculty development opportunities speak to the desirability of cross-curricular projects that engage faculty in evaluating some aspect(s) of the curriculum at work. At WSU and Carleton, differing concerns arose about students' writing competencies; hence, a writing portfolio provided a good vehicle not only to address that perceived weakness but also to engage faculty in thinking about students' successes and failures as results of their course work. That, in turn, engages faculty in exploring solutions together.

Equally important as sites of faculty learning are those opportunities that arise from the routine work of the institution. These opportunities have a different social context and draw different participants. In fact, most if not all faculty participate in this work. For those also participating in formal activities it enriches their learning. For those who are not participating in formal activities it is an essential source of information about teaching and the norms that are present on campus. Capitalizing on the reach of routine opportunities with designs that intentionally support faculty learning in addition to completion of work could be a powerful avenue. Carleton's design of the portfolio rating events is a case in point—explored more fully in later chapters.

As this volume continues, more specific effects will be presented, showing a range of faculty development opportunities and suggesting ways of establishing, promoting, and exploiting them for students' benefit. For now, comparing these two institutions' efforts reveals some good news in and of itself. Small or large, institutions can mount successful efforts. Whether the central administration is supportive or not, faculty can find ways of improving their teaching practices. Even in the absence of a budget for faculty development, institutions can engage faculty in initiatives that provide implicit forms of faculty development and thus get more for their money when carrying out activities that count for accreditation, accountability, or assessment. Looking for at least one "common cause" activity is clearly important. Such an activity—like Critical Thinking at WSU or QuIRK at Carleton—can provide formal faculty development. At Carleton, a routine activity—portfolio rating—is conceived and constructed as an opportunity for formal faculty development. But as observed on the WSU campus, that same kind of assessment activity acts as powerful routine development while accomplishing an important institutional goal.

3 Seeking the Evidence

THE PROJECT WAS named the Tracer Project to reflect its goal of tracing the effects of faculty development through changes in practice to an impact on student learning. As shown in figure 3.1, in its simplest form, this conceptualization can be envisioned as a direct path, one that can be understood by exploring the change in faculty attitudes and knowledge during the development activity, the change in their instruction that follows, and the change in the quantity or type of learning demonstrated by their students. The model has been briefly, and perhaps unconsciously, described by Angelo and Cross: "The quality of student learning is directly, although not exclusively, related to the quality of teaching. Therefore, one of the most promising ways to improve learning is to improve teaching" (1993).

Since the model was first proposed by Donald Kirkpatrick (1959), it has been widely adopted in human resource development training over the last fifty years (Hilbert, Preskill, and Russ-Eft 1997; Alliger et al. 1997; Kirkpatrick 2010). Desimone (2009) proposed using this model as a core conceptual framework for studying professional development of K–12 teachers. She notes that its strength is that it embodies a direct and testable theory for how professional development leads to changes in student learning. The Tracer Project embraced this model for designing the study, capitalizing on its clarity to focus data collection and analysis in order to demonstrate that faculty development does indeed lead to faculty learning, which translates to changes in classroom instruction that impact student learning. This model proposes the Direct Path from faculty learning to student learning.

However, most educators know that learning is much more complex than going to class, learning something, and applying it. Prior knowledge, motivation to learn, interactions with other learners, and the challenges of transfer to new situations for our students also matter (Bransford, Brown, and Cocking 2000). These contextual variables, Desimone acknowledges, are just as important for teacher learning, and in our case for faculty learning. Thus, the Tracer team added a second approach to studying professional development on both campuses—one that used ethnographic

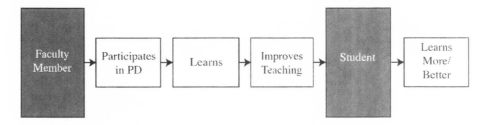

Figure 3.1. The Direct Path model shows a simple logic model connecting professional faculty development (PD) to improved student learning.

methods to provide a more holistic view of faculty development: who participated, why, what their experience was with faculty development, how this experience fit into other learning experiences on campus and off, what faculty did with their new knowledge, how it worked, what accelerators and barriers helped or hindered improvement, how teaching and faculty understanding evolved over time, and what faculty perceptions of impact arose. This contextual view, which is referred to as a situated learning perspective by other educational researchers (Putnam and Borko 2000; Borko 2004; Webster-Wright 2009), expanded an understanding of both the experiences that come together to change instruction and the impacts of faculty development beyond the individual. By using a systems perspective to faculty development (see figure 3.2), the study could examine the process of social participation in learning and collective changes in practice (Lave and Wenger 1991; Cobb and Bowers 1999). Bringing both approaches together allowed for stronger statements about the efficacy of the simpler model while developing a more nuanced understanding of how faculty learning takes place. The contextual study examines the existing culture of teaching and learning on a campus, which places the Direct Path model into its fuller institutional context.

Studying the Direct Path

One of the strengths of the Direct Path as a theoretical frame for evaluating professional development is the clarity with which it identifies points where studies can be focused and data collected. In fact, there is a long history of studying segments of the Direct Path both within K–12 and undergraduate contexts. Numerous studies of faculty development activities have used exit surveys to collect information on faculty satisfaction. In recent years, these have focused more heavily on faculty learning in formal workshops (Bunce, Havanki, and VandenPlas 2008; Pfund et al., 2009; Felder and Brent 2010), and many studies have looked at the impact on teaching from both self-report and observational data (Budd et al. 2013; Ebert-May et al. 2011; Fisher et al. 2010). The impact of teaching methods on student learning is a rich area of research

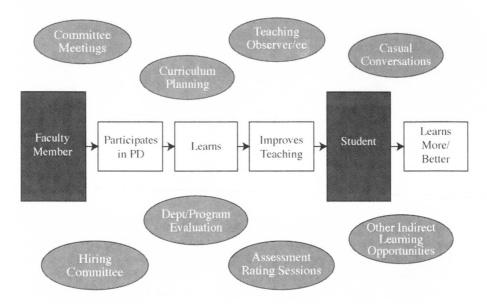

Figure 3.2. The Context Model places the Direct Path model in the broader context of the campus culture of teaching and learning. Bubbles show that faculty learning opportunities about teaching occur in a range of circumstances that can interact with learning connected to a specific professional development experience. An individual faculty member may contribute to as well as learn from these opportunities, extending the influence of a specific professional development event and complicating interpretation of its direct impact on teaching.

both in education (Fisher et al. 2010; Fishman et al. 2003) and in discipline-based education research (Singer, Nielsen, and Schweingruber 2012). However, in both educational contexts, studying the full pathway from faculty development to student learning is rare. Studying the Direct Path requires identifying strategies for studying each of the three critical steps in the path:

1. Do faculty learn as intended at the professional development workshops?
2. Do they translate this learning into their teaching?
3. Does the improved teaching lead to improved learning?

None of these three questions is trivial to answer; however, researchers on both campuses had the advantage of being able to study well-established professional development activities that had been initiated years in the past, allowing an examination of the long-term effect from development experiences. At Carleton these programs are still in place, allowing collection of information on current participants in programs as well as the opportunity to study the immediate impacts. On both campuses, faculty assignments associated with these programs are collected routinely as part of campus-wide assessments of students' writing skills, providing a set of artifacts that allowed data collection to move beyond self-reporting and to look at changes over time. Student work generated from these assignments is also collected through the two campuses' writing portfolios, thus completing the chain from professional development to student learning.

Building on these opportunities, the project sought to obtain information combining an understanding of faculty perceptions about their teaching (self-report data) with information that allowed for direct observation of change either through analysis of assignments or student work, or through observations of teaching. This combination is powerful because on the one hand it probes the faculty members' thinking about their teaching and development experiences, and on the other hand it allows analysis of artifacts and observations to guide interpretation of these reflections (Greene, Caracelli, and Graham 1989). Student learning was measured through structured analysis of student work. The research team did not attempt to collect student views on their learning. Most of the student work analyzed had been completed in the past, making interviews difficult, and such an approach would have expanded the project to unmanageable scope. Other studies have demonstrated the complexity of student learning (Bransford, Brown, and Cocking 2000). Tracer, therefore, sought only to demonstrate that a signal could be measured.

At both WSU and Carleton, previous research has established links between faculty learning and student learning. At WSU, the Critical Thinking Project (1999–2003) revealed that when faculty adopted an approach based on their own adaptation of WSU's Guide to Rating Critical Thinking, students in their classes outperformed students in similar classes where the teacher was not using the same approach, as well as students in earlier versions of that same teacher's course. Research conducted under a three-year grant from the Fund for the Improvement of Post-Secondary Education (FIPSE) established that when a teacher learns better practices for establishing expectations about critical thinking and changes her course to reflect that learning, students' performances improve substantially, using Pearson's Correlation Coefficient, ($p < .01$). In addition, a comparison between students' performances in multi-section courses, where some teachers used the critical thinking methodologies (freely adapted by individual teachers) and other teachers taught the course as they wished but without faculty development in critical thinking, reveals similarly significant gains in learning when faculty undergo development for incorporating critical thinking into their pedagogy ($p < .01$). Thus, in WSU's critical thinking project, when faculty learned better practices for teaching students to think critically, students responded by improving the quality of their thinking in their written products (Kelly-Riley et al. 2001; Monroe 2003; Brown, Smith, and Henderson 2007).

At Carleton, early portfolio research established a direct connection between the number of faculty development events a teacher had attended and the likelihood that a student would choose a paper from that teacher's course for the student's writing portfolio (Rutz and Lauer-Glebov 2005). In effect, students' portfolio selections amounted to an endorsement of their teachers' best practices in designing assignments, scaffolding the writing process, and responding to students' writing—all prominent aspects of Carleton's Writing Across the Curriculum (WAC) faculty development.

Moving forward from this foundation, researchers understood that the details of data collection and analysis would need to be distinct on the two campuses, each of which presented different opportunities to collect data given the differences in timelines and scales of implementation of professional development activities. Further, the goals and strategies of the programs were distinct, requiring differences in the analysis. In general, however, data collection and analysis techniques associated with each of the primary research questions generated from the Direct Path framework took place as follows.

Do Faculty Learn as Intended at the Faculty Development Workshops?

This question was studied only at Carleton, as the critical thinking project was completed prior to the initiation of our research project. Carleton used workshop exit surveys to obtain self-reported changes in attitude, skills, and knowledge and leader interviews to understand the desired outcomes of the workshop. The survey and interview data were analyzed using the intended goals as a framework to understand if learning was aligned with these goals and to characterize the nature of the learning.

Do Faculty Translate This Learning into Their Teaching?

This question lies at the heart of the study and required a combination of interviews, analysis of assignments, and observations to attack it. While it appears that a relatively straightforward design would be possible—collecting and comparing assignments prior to and following the workshop—this approach is confounded in numerous ways. Faculty may or may not repeat their assignments from term to term, nor do they remember very accurately what they did in the past. Faculty change their assignments—or not—in response to numerous influences ranging from the time available for assignment development at a particular point in the term, to the past experiences of students in the classroom, to a change in the course content. Often when they change an assignment, they also change major elements of the course at the same time. Thus, even when before-and-after samples were obtainable, in many cases it was difficult to directly compare assignments before and after the professional development event.

In order to allow quantitative comparison of the strength of assignment elements that were targeted by faculty development, a rubric-based scoring by multiple faculty members was implemented. This technique was pioneered at Washington State University in earlier studies (Condon and Kelly-Riley 2004). Initially, both Carleton and Washington State University assignments were scored using the Critical Thinking

Assignment Rubric. While this rubric provided robust measures of the strength of assignments aligned with the goals of WSU faculty development, Carleton assignments were not as sensitive to this rubric, as the goals of the professional development at Carleton differed in substantive ways. Carleton researchers therefore developed a strategy for comparing assignments based on the Haswell method (1988) that used a rubric specifically aligned with the goals of professional development as articulated by leaders in response to the investigation of workshop goals.

On both campuses, researchers also collected rich qualitative data from faculty describing changes they made in their teaching and teachers' perceived relationship of changes to professional development experiences. These data provide a bridge between an analysis of the Direct Path and the larger cultural context of faculty learning on campus and its effects on teaching.

Does the Improved Teaching Lead to Improved Student Learning?

Efforts to analyze student learning focused on analyzing writing produced in response to assignments before and after faculty development. This strategy was appropriate for many reasons, first and foremost being that the faculty development programs on both campuses were primarily directed at improving the quality of writing assignments that caused students to improve either their critical thinking, their quantitative reasoning, or their writing.

Focusing on writing assignments made use of the extensive collections of student writing that have been gathered over time in student portfolios used to evaluate students' writing proficiency. This is not a complete collection of all faculty assignments or of the responses of all students in a class to a single assignment at a particular point in time. However, it provides a large sample of student work in response to assignments developed by many faculty through time. Attempts to collect more complete sets of student work proved futile.

As the writing portfolios serve as graduation requirements at both institutions, they carry considerable curricular importance. At WSU, portfolios represent the students' analysis of the best writing that students have completed in the first two years of college. Work was included in the portfolio only if the students felt that they had responded well to the assignment. At Carleton, students must choose writing and associated assignments that meet specific rhetorical tasks, which may or may not correspond to students' sense of their best work. Regardless, this self-selection allowed us to see how a range of students responded to an assignment, while eliminating writing that students understood was not living up to their own expectations for one reason or another. Portfolio data exist for all undergraduate students on both campuses, thus yielding a sample that is not biased by student achievement or faculty perceptions of success in their course.

Both Carleton and WSU have used the portfolios extensively to understand learning on campus (Condon and Kelly-Riley 2004; Rutz and Lauer-Glebov 2005). Because portfolio assessment is central to institutional-level assessment, published results describing writing on campus could be used to contextualize the findings of the current study. Further, several of the professional development activities studied in this project arose from studies of portfolio work that identified critical weaknesses in student learning beyond writing: in critical thinking at WSU (Hamp-Lyons and Condon 2000; Condon and Kelly-Riley 2004) and in quantitative reasoning at Carleton (Rutz and Grawe 2009).

As with the faculty assignments, rubric-based scoring by multiple faculty was used to assess student work. Scorers were trained on the rubric, with two readers scoring each paper; discrepancies greater than 6, on the total score for all dimensions, were resolved through discussion among readers. These rating strategies were initially used to score work from both Carleton and WSU.

This approach yielded valuable results for WSU student writing, where the rubric is well aligned with the professional development program under study. In a finding similar to that for the assignments themselves, Carleton student writing was less sensitive to the rubric. In particular, a low-scoring assignment prompt did not predict low-scoring student work, and ratings showed no significant differences across work in many categories. Thus the Carleton team developed a comparison rubric for student writing based on Richard Haswell's inter-subject paired comparison method (1988).[1] As was the case for the assignment rubric, this rubric was aligned with the specific goals of the faculty development effort as described by the leaders of the professional development program (Willett, Iverson, Rutz, and Manduca 2014). At two separate rating sessions at Carleton, raters analyzed two student work samples from the same assignment or two assignment prompts of similar nature. Raters did not know which paper or prompt was written earlier than the other, and they did not have access to information on course, student, or faculty identities. Nevertheless, through direct comparison of two papers or two prompts on specific analytic measures related to faculty development goals, raters helped to detect changes that holistic ratings might not register.[2]

Understanding the Larger Context

The study of the Direct Path (see figure 3.1) was situated within a contextual study aimed at obtaining a more holistic picture of faculty development and its impacts on both campuses. The range of skills, techniques, and approaches that one institution's faculty bring to the classroom, coupled with the students' highly varied previous experiences, knowledge, and abilities, creates an enormously complex mixture of possibilities. Given all the possible influences on teaching and learning, how can one identify with any certainty that *this* student's gain was the result of *this* change in a professor's teaching practice, or that *this* change in a professor's teaching practice was a result of *this* professional development activity? Addressing these questions required combining ethnographic techniques with the data analysis described above to investigate the experiences of significant populations of faculty on both campuses—both those who had participated extensively in faculty development and those who had not.

In pursuing inferences about faculty and student learning, then, the study took certain principles as axiomatic:

- Learning—for faculty and for students—is longitudinal. It happens over time, and progress is neither uniform nor standardized.
- Measurements need to be aggregated and must observe learning over time, whenever possible, rather than only at a given point.
- Learning happens everywhere and all the time, not merely in one time or one place.
- Measurements need to capture progress along identified dimensions (e.g., critical thinking, writing, quantitative reasoning, etc.) over time, and across multiple exposures.
- Learning is far more than an accumulation of facts.
- Instruments measuring significant learning have to balance the need to reach serious, continuing, higher-order learning impacts with the need to identify specific results in learning outcomes.

The scale of these studies is not at the level of the individual instructor but at the scale of the institution, as well as being longitudinal and always mindful of context. Interviews, observations, and other methods have to reasonably account for cumulative effects, tracing them to likely sources, and using multiple methodologies to establish the likelihood that students' learning is the result of changes identified in the learning process or environment. Under the best conditions, these changes produce a steady, identifiable progression in those processes and that environment. The methods must be capable of detecting and accommodating that continuing evolution.

As was the case for study of the Direct Path, differences in context and particularly scale shaped these studies of the larger context. At Carleton, researchers were able to sit in on and observe a set of courses, conduct extensive interviews with the faculty and students in those courses, and collect course materials and student work products. Indeed, the faculty members being observed looked at their participation as a kind of privilege, rather than as a burden. The combination of the researchers' expertise and the closeness of a small campus allowed for rich ethnographic research of the effects of faculty development on the faculty members' practices and on students' learning opportunities.

The story was different at WSU; there, the large campus tends to isolate people—and expertise—in silos. The sense of community that exists at Carleton is found in different places at WSU, where communities generally form within departments or, in the case of small departments, within schools or colleges. Few WSU faculty saw any intrinsic reason to participate in the Tracer Project, leading researchers to establish a system of payment for faculty participation. For an honorarium of $150, 168 faculty members agreed to (1) provide researchers with copies of a syllabus and all assignment materials for one course, (2) provide a set of student responses to a course assignment, and (3) meet with a research assistant for a 30–45 minute interview about their teaching practices—in particular, for most, about the effects of various faculty development events on their practices.

On both campuses, investigators compared the teaching of faculty who had participated with varying degrees of enthusiasm in varying kinds and amounts of faculty development. Both campuses were successful in sampling faculty who had participated extensively and those who had participated very little, groups characterized as high and low participators. Both campus contexts also allowed examination of long trajectories of faculty learning and its impact on teaching. Thus, in addition to looking at short-term, direct effects of faculty development, the data reveal cumulative effects of development through time and long-term effects of faculty development in the distant past. Perhaps most interesting was the vast array of ways in which faculty learn about teaching on two very different campuses. These features of both data sets allow for important conclusions about faculty learning and student learning.

Sample and Data Collection at WSU

WSU began by looking for faculty from established faculty development projects: in particular, fifty faculty who had been through at least one two-day WAC workshop, fifty who had participated in the FIPSE-sponsored Critical Thinking Project, and, in an attempt to ask whether an activity like rating Junior Writing Portfolios really did serve as a kind of faculty development, forty faculty who regularly served as portfolio raters. WSU researchers thought of this activity as faculty development grounded in routine events because it afforded raters the opportunity to see the kinds of writing tasks to which students responded well, to focus on the differences in writing tasks and kinds of writing among the disciplines, and to discuss with each other faculty standards for "good writing." At WSU, portfolio rating is not constructed to include faculty development as a purpose or outcome of the activity, but researchers hypothesized that it nevertheless produced such effects. Finally, on neither campus could researchers identify a traditional control group of faculty who had not participated in any faculty development activity (Rutz et al. 2012). All faculty had participated in specifying learning outcomes for their departments' concentrations and graduate programs; almost all had participated in some kind of assessment of those programs, if only in the service of WSU's 2009 accreditation process. In short, in one way or another, all faculty participate in some activity that involves discussing student performance and defining success. Hence, the *comparison* group at WSU consisted of 28 faculty members classified as "low participating." They participated in activities that, in effect, came to them—a teaching-focused departmental workshop or colloquium, for example. Tables 3.1a, 3.1b, and 3.1c describe the faculty subjects from WSU.

TABLE 3.1A. DISTRIBUTION OF FACULTY PARTICIPANTS AT WASHINGTON STATE UNIVERSITY

LOW-PARTICIPATING FACULTY (3 OR FEWER EVENTS/YEAR)	HIGH-PARTICIPATING FACULTY (4 OR MORE EVENTS/YEAR)
28	140

TABLE 3.1B. DISTRIBUTION OF FACULTY PARTICIPANTS AT WASHINGTON STATE UNIVERSITY (CONTINUED)

CRITICAL THINKING PROJECT PARTICIPANTS	WAC WORKSHOP PARTICIPANTS	PORTFOLIO RATERS	LOW-PARTICIPATING FACULTY
50	50	40	28

TABLE 3.1C. DISTRIBUTION OF FACULTY PARTICIPANTS AT WASHINGTON STATE UNIVERSITY (CONTINUED)

ADJUNCT	CONTINUING, NON-TENURE TRACK	TENURE TRACK
16	40	114

Faculty participants came from every school and college. Adjuncts and non-tenure track participants were also drawn from across the curriculum, though about half were concentrated in two important undergraduate programs: composition (a one-semester universal requirement at WSU) and World Civilizations (a two-course universal requirement, since replaced, which served as the anchor for WSU's previous General Education Program). Since WSU has also recently (during the Tracer Project's research period) abolished its Center for Teaching, Learning, and Technology (CTLT), WSU researchers decided to recruit participants from specific faculty development activities that were not sponsored by CTLT, though many of those participants also attended CTLT events while that unit still existed.

In addition, since the Tracer Project was interested in gathering data about the longitudinal effects of faculty development, WSU subjects were drawn from faculty who had been teaching at WSU for at least ten years. As a whole, by 2004,

- more than 300 faculty had undergone a year-long process of incorporating critical thinking into their courses
  - critical-thinking faculty had improved their assignments
  - students in the classes of these faculty had improved their performances on critical-thinking assessments
- approximately 1,200 faculty had attended at least one two-day WAC workshop focused on improving writing assignments
- more than 350 faculty had trained to be portfolio raters
- 28 faculty were selected to represent low-participating faculty: those who participated in three or fewer events per year and who did not seek out opportunities for development

Over a two-year period, WSU researchers interviewed these 168 instructional faculty about their experiences with faculty development and how those experiences affected their teaching practices; collected and analyzed assignments, syllabi, and student work products from those faculty members' classes; and conducted critical-thinking rating sessions on those student work products. The subject group, as a whole, is quite representative of the faculty at large. The range of attention they pay to teaching and the time they spend working on it is also typical of the practices of WSU faculty.

WSU's Critical Thinking Project

Between 1999 and 2003, a team of WSU faculty developers worked for at least a year at a time with 350 faculty, helping them explore the most productive ways of building critical thinking into their course assignments. Faculty began by adapting WSU's *Guide to Rating Critical and Integrative Thinking* (see appendix 1) to fit their disciplines and the levels of their students. Then they redesigned one course to incorporate critical thinking as a principal learning outcome. Their participation lasted through two iterations of that course, during which time they were also trained to rate students' work according to the original *Guide,* and they gave a presentation or workshop about their work to faculty in their home departments.

The Tracer Project set out to discover (1) whether that intensive faculty development had persisted in the faculty members' courses, (2) whether faculty had continued to experiment and innovate in the years since the Critical Thinking Project ended, and (3) whether the effects were still measurable in their students' work. Researchers collected syllabi and assignments in order to analyze them for continuing influences of the Critical Thinking Project and for evidence of expansion or further development since that time. Each faculty member also provided a set of student responses to a course assignment, and those assignment prompts and student samples were rated using the process employed during the Critical Thinking Project.

Once the course materials were analyzed, each faculty member was interviewed, responding to the following questions:

1. How often do you change your course syllabus or assignment materials?
2. When you do make changes, what are the most important influences prompting you to do so?
3. What faculty development events have you attended in the past two years?
4. What changes have you made in your teaching practices as a result?
5. What other events have you attended (department or committee meetings, webinars, conferences, lectures, etc.) that have had an impact on your teaching?
6. Do you feel that your department and college value your participation in faculty development activities? Why or why not?
7. How do you think your students have responded to the changes you have made?
8. Have you written about or made a presentation about your work in the classroom, locally, regionally, or nationally? If so, what was it about?
9. Can you identify one significant change you made in the course you are sharing with us, and identify the source of your decision to make that change?

Finally, the assignment prompts and the student work samples were independently rated by faculty whom the researchers trained to use the *Guide to Rating Critical and Integrative Thinking*. Scores were given on each of seven dimensions, using a six-point scale ranging from "absent" to "mastering." In addition, researchers queried the Writing Portfolio database about students' submissions from these faculty members' classes.

Writing Portfolio Raters

For some time, the people who administer the Junior Writing Portfolio have suspected that rater trainings and rating sessions were performing some kind of faculty development function, even though these events do not explicitly aim to improve raters' teaching practices. Forty portfolio raters were recruited and went through the same procedures described above, in order to discover whether the activities and the faculty learning involved in rating portfolios produced changes in the raters' teaching practices that could be discerned using our methods for tracing effects into student learning outcomes.

WAC Workshop Participants

Each year since 1987, WSU has offered a two-day WAC workshop as part of the institution's support for its two-course Writing in the Major requirement. Over that time span, more than 1,200 faculty have participated in at least one workshop; however, since these faculty tend to be more senior in rank, and because WSU experiences a high turnover rate in faculty at advanced rank, fewer than 150 faculty participants are still teaching at WSU at any one time. Fifty WAC faculty participated as subjects and provided the same set of materials as the critical thinking faculty. WAC faculty also sat for the same interviews, and their courses were also queried in the portfolio database, as described above.

Low-Participating Faculty

Low-participating faculty are those teachers who attended three or fewer events per year that provided some form of faculty development. At WSU, these faculty described such events as "coming to them": workshops, lectures, or colloquia sponsored by their own departments, in the case of formal development; or routine departmental or committee meetings concerned with setting or measuring learning outcomes in the department's undergraduate concentrations or graduate programs, meetings that often provided insights about teaching. Again, document collection, interviewing, ratings, and portfolio database queries proceeded as above. Comparisons allowed for conclusions about whether the effects identified in high-participating faculty members' students resulted from those teachers' practices or were part of the larger teaching and learning environment at WSU.

Data Gathering at Carleton

At Carleton, sampling began with faculty who had attended WAC and quantitative reasoning workshops and/or who had rated sophomore writing portfolios. The sample soon grew to include participants in lunch events and winter workshops sponsored by the College's Perlman Center for Learning and Teaching (LTC). Attendance indicated departments where faculty development likely was taking hold. In 2010, more than half of the 234 instructional faculty employed at Carleton attended a winter workshop and/or at least one of the almost weekly LTC lunch activities.

Guided by inferences drawn from these high-participating faculty and a knowledge about ongoing initiatives, the team used different methods to get at the different scale and context at Carleton: both the smaller size of the faculty population and the established commitment to teaching and learning on the campus (Singer and Rutz 2004) suggested a selection of methodologies that included ethnographic approaches. Over a period of three years, a mixture of quantitative and qualitative methodologies were used and a wide range of sources were accessed in order to search for overlapping patterns (or themes) in student and faculty experience of teaching and learning. In other words, within limits, this triangulation of data and materials helped to create a picture of Carleton's institutional approaches to teaching and learning. Methods included interviews, surveys, participant-observation, and writing (or discourse) analysis (see appendix for complete list). These methods helped illuminate the range and depth of individuals' experiences and explain results from the quantitative methods related to faculty development, teaching, and learning. The iterative process of this approach allowed patterns to emerge and suggested additional participant areas of inquiry.

Interviews, Surveys, and Participant Observations

Different types of interviews and different sampling strategies helped piece together a more complete picture of the culture of teaching and learning and its potential influence on student learning. The study explored faculty motivations to participate and institutional practices and discourse related to teaching and learning. Data collection reflected faculty change and how these changes might be manifested in artifacts, such as syllabi and assignment prompts. Eighty interviews captured perceptions from a diverse set of faculty, staff, administrators, and some students across the curriculum, across age ranges, and across seniority and leadership roles (47 instructional faculty are included in this number). Responses were compared with the responses to surveys from seventeen Winter Workshops (from 2009 to 2011) in order to confirm (or question) the project's hypotheses.

Participant observations provided an even clearer picture of teaching and learning and of the kinds of faculty experiences available. Participant observations came from faculty development activities (workshops, LTC lunches, portfolio rating sessions, and various faculty and staff retreats), classroom observation of a set of five freshmen seminar courses, and ongoing campus and student life activities. These observations provided crucial information about the extent to which—and ways in which—faculty, staff, and students engaged in learning activities on campus. Everyday interactions with people on campus also helped obtain key support for interviews, survey participation, and rating project participation.

Classroom Case Studies

The sets of observations from five freshmen seminars in the fall term of 2010 provided context for the faculty interviews, student surveys, and artifact ratings. Structured observations documented the "magical moments" of teaching (Singer and Rutz 2004) that were not visible in the quantitative data from surveys and rating sessions. Assignments and student work from these five courses indicated that the goals of faculty development were reflected in the assignments themselves as well as in the student work—even for first-term, first-year students.

Drawing Conclusions from Diverse Data

Both campuses yielded rich data that included observations of campus-wide events, customs, and culture, broad exploration of faculty and student experience, and deep exploration of the experiences of specific faculty or classrooms. To bring these observations together, the team as a whole used a variety of techniques drawn from social science and educational research. Rich characterizations were developed from the data of key informant interviews, observation, and discourse analysis. These data were triangulated with action research data from current faculty development activities and the quantitative analysis obtained through the rubric-based rating sessions of student work and assignment prompts.

On neither campus could the Tracer team identify a group of faculty who had not participated in some formal faculty development (Rutz et al. 2012). Hence, this study does not make use of an experimental design identifying a treatment group and a control group. Rather, it is grounded in a situated learning perspective (Putnam and Borko 2000; Webster-Wright 2009) that allows for a systems approach to understanding the different experiences of faculty and ways in which experiences that lead to productive changes in their teaching can be amplified.

Discoveries about Methodologies

The combination of studying both the Direct Path and the broader context helped to understand the impact of faculty development, particularly its effects on faculty, on both campuses. Without the focusing effects of the Direct Path study, there could be no structured insights on impacts of workshops on teaching. Without the contextual study, there could be no inferences about the importance of informal learning opportunities and the spread of effect beyond individual faculty.

Framing the study as a combination of measures of the Direct Path and contextual effects also provided flexibility, allowing the project to use different measures at the two institutions, measures that were appropriate to their histories and contexts while providing structure that allowed comparisons of data across institutions. Other institutions will find the need to use their own strategies for understanding the learning that takes place at faculty development events, the impact of this learning on instruction, the impact on students, and the broader context in which these three steps operate. However, research at two institutions as different as Carleton College and Washington State University suggests that this framing will be both productive within the institution and in allowing comparisons between institutions.

While the Carleton paired rating system for assessing student work differed markedly from the procedures that had long been used and thoroughly tested at WSU, the differences stemmed from characteristics of the student samples themselves and from differences between the two institutions. One of the inferences from this experience is that this kind of evaluation resembles research more than it resembles some kind of pan-institutional evaluation. Researchers must gather data as broadly and purposefully as possible, and they must bring to bear responsible tools of analysis. But they must also be aware that the standard application of a rigid tool is unlikely to provide useful information—at least not across one institution or between institutions. Therefore, researchers must be willing to try different tools, to experiment further in response to early failure, to count progress toward making an analysis as success in progress.

Perhaps most important, the Tracer Project needed to begin where the research team had expertise and where the student outcomes could be readily obtained. For these two institutions, that meant focusing on writing portfolios. For other institutions, an archive of student work products may lie elsewhere, in a writing center, in departmental samples, in an office of institutional research. But without actual student work products or an understanding of the research team's particular expertise, drawing connections between what a school's faculty is teaching and what its students are learning becomes a far more intractable challenge. Such an analysis must be embedded in local outcomes, local curricula, and actual course work. So, if a campus does not already have an archive already, it must start one.

Similarly, the focus of analysis must track the faculty's use of pedagogies as promoted in the school's faculty development. Despite some surprising similarities between WSU and Carleton, the focus of faculty development differed on the two campuses, so the kinds of data researchers could collect differed, and so did the kinds of analysis they could perform. There is nothing generic about this work. It must be tailored to each local context—though clearly some methods can be broadly adapted so that many institutions can use them, and, just as clearly, researchers should cast an eye toward results that can be compared among institutions.

Whenever an institution sets out to track students' learning, a longitudinal study will yield more data than a "snapshot." Since learning is complex, takes place everywhere, and requires time to solidify, the snapshot lacks the ability to tell a story about faculty development and students' learning. At the very least, a series of snapshots taken over time is necessary for comparison, in order to discover whether progress is being made. Even better, using and triangulating from a range of quantitative and qualitative methods allows researchers to view the same pieces from different perspectives, thus providing a richer picture of dynamic whole. Including in these methods an archive of student work samples over time, an archive that yields data about faculty development initiatives, allows for far richer inferences—and more productive changes. Tracking change is a complex, ongoing project, not a one-time study.

Along those same lines, different campus cultures lead to differing measures, even for the same kind of process—for example, rating student artifacts. At WSU, a relative few raters are selected and trained to rate samples from across the university. In a given year, for example, approximately 40 faculty members rate 4,400 writing portfolios. At WSU, 2 percent of the faculty provide a service for the other 98 percent. At Carleton, approximately 35 faculty annually rate roughly 450 portfolios: 17 percent of the faculty participate, which changes the visibility and the impact of Carleton's portfolio on its campus. In approaching methods for using portfolio data to make discoveries about student learning, such differences matter. Portfolio rating counts as a routine site for faculty learning at WSU, but as a formal site for faculty development at Carleton. Understanding the differences shapes the research.

Understanding changes in a community demands a more holistic approach, acknowledging the dynamic context (Weiss 2002; Webster-Wright 2009; Patton 2011). The Tracer Project examined the underlying assumptions and activities for the faculty development program and attempted to trace a path through the linkages. The team's approach recognized the nature of the complex educational system. While this chapter describes possible methods other campuses can try, it also functions as permission to find other methods more suitable to local contexts, to the campus culture, and the many other factors examined in this chapter—and more. Faculty members are all under pressure to specify what students are learning and to establish transparently that good teaching matters to faculty and that good teaching results in powerful learning. Those outside (and sometimes inside) the academy seek more generic tools that take snapshots of learning. This research counteracts these measures by developing context-sensitive methods that provide sound systematic inquiry and that are integrated into an institution's curriculum. Differences in campus environments present challenges, but this study has shown that those differences also create different opportunities on each campus.

Results of this research demonstrate the need for more, larger, and better studies of faculty learning as it affects student learning. While this study spanned more than three years and included a wide variety of methods, other institutions will inevitably experiment with their own versions of this work by following some of the lessons learned here: (1) local mission, learning outcomes, and pedagogical practices must provide the criteria for this analysis; (2) assessing new practice or technological innovation requires careful attention to the goals of the faculty development activities; and (3) over the long haul, students benefit from institutional support for faculty learners. In short, deciding what to measure and choosing the instruments are equally important to maintain a focus on student learning.

4 Faculty Learning Applied

THIS CHAPTER EXPLORES the first links in the chain between professional development and improved student learning: the impact of professional development on faculty knowledge, skills, and attitudes and the subsequent changes in their teaching that result as they apply their learning.

The chapter begins with a look at the most direct effects as described in the Direct Path, including the impact of workshops, portfolio rating, and other formal or routine occasions available for faculty learning. Is there a difference in the assignments developed by faculty who have participated in professional development activities? Do these changes reflect the intended outcomes of the workshop? The perspective then broadens to situate these observations in the larger cultures of the two campuses. What is the motivation for faculty to attend to their teaching? How do motivation, status, and reward play into the changes they make?

Step 1: Faculty Learning in Formal Workshops

Exploring faculty learning in formal workshops allows a determination of whether the workshops lead to the intended effect. The workshop itself is the first place that the Direct Path can break down. Just as students can develop misconceptions in our classes, so too can faculty leave formal workshops without developing the new knowledge, skills, and attitudes that the workshop fostered. This study was able to explore learning during such workshops only at Carleton, as the WSU workshop program is no longer in place.

Matching self-reported learning gains at the end of workshops offered in winter 2009 and 2010 with the goals of the workshop leaders showed strong alignment between the knowledge and skills the instructors were aiming to develop and the knowledge and skills faculty perceived they were developing. While this may seem a trivial measure, there are numerous examples for students (Denofrio et al. 2007; Hagay and Baram-Tsabari 2011) and faculty (Henderson, Beach, and Finkelstein 2011) where this is not the case. In the Carleton case, faculty reported that the primary outcomes of a Writing with Numbers workshop (which was originally offered in 2005 and repeated by popular demand in 2007 and 2010) were well aligned with both the goal of the faculty development opportunity and the campus initiatives of Writing Across the Curriculum (WAC) and Quantitative Inquiry, Reasoning, and Knowledge (QuIRK). Eighteen participants responded to a survey following the 2010 workshop, noting

- the importance of using assignments that scaffold learning through revision of multiple drafts
- the use of rubrics to communicate the standard for success in the writing assignment
- the value of short and effective comments
- the need for students to experiment with different types of writing

Faculty participating in a workshop on developing quantitative reasoning left believing that it was important to give students learning opportunities and feedback that

- prompted them to develop quantitative reasoning as a habit of mind
- encouraged precision in writing about quantitative writing and discouraged the use of imprecise language such as "many," "some," or "most"
- allowed them to work with primary data sources to develop quantitative skills

Participants also left understanding that staff, student consultants, and prefects on campus were resources that could help them and their students develop quantitative reasoning skills.

These themes are central to the goals of the professional development opportunities at Carleton, so this finding provides confidence in the outcomes of the workshop and identifies knowledge that is available to faculty participants for application in their teaching.

Observations of the workshops, survey responses, and discussions with faculty at Carleton shed light on the factors that contributed to the success of the workshops in facilitating the desired learning. Like their students, faculty and staff most often learn better from experiential activities. Faculty repeatedly expressed preferences in workshop surveys and interviews for programs in which they could actively work on designing an assignment, course syllabus, or other aspect of pedagogy. Hence, workshops integrated time and activities for faculty to begin to design new assignments or courses. The 2009–2011 winter workshops for new faculty provided time for participants to observe, critique, and conduct micro-teaching (fifteen minutes) lessons for the group and to spend time with a partner discussing a syllabus that they were designing. Workshops like Writing with Numbers in 2010 required participants to begin to design an assignment as preparation for the program and then to revise it in the course of the workshop. Although not all of these assignments were classroom-ready after the workshop, the activity helped participants better understand how they could directly apply what they were learning in the workshop to their own courses. In this particular workshop, participants took away a wide range of ideas about what they hoped to change in their teaching: using more mini-assignments, collaborating with colleagues on teaching, using grading rubrics, incorporating peer review, making better use of group projects, understanding different disciplinary approaches and uses for posters, designing assignments around problems, incorporating more pre-writing and exploratory writing, grading faster, diversifying the types of writing assignments in the course, and including assignments with quantitative reasoning components. This workshop design applies best practices in learning to the faculty setting. Learning outcomes are clearly aligned with workshop design; participants are engaged in learning from one another; they have an opportunity to practice the skills they are developing and receive feedback; and they leave having initiated transfer of this new learning to their own classrooms. Such designs are well regarded by faculty and known to impact learning (Narum and Manduca 2012; Felder and Brent 2010; Bunce, Havanki, and VandenPlas 2008; Manduca et al. 2005).

Similar results were recorded in interview data from the New Faculty Winter Workshops (NFWW, 2009–2011), where new faculty are enculturated in teaching and learning at Carleton. Participants reported plans for social networking and internet technologies (in Moodle), new writing assignments (based on discussions with the director of the Writing Program), new approaches to engaging students in discussion, the use of grading rubrics, and scaffolding assignments into their courses better, among many other pedagogical topics. The majority of NFWW participants confidently described their interest in trying out new pedagogies, exemplified in these comments below:

- "I'm less worried trying new things or experimenting with ideas and assignments" (2009 NFWW survey participant).
- "Less is more. I really want to return to using pedagogic techniques that I used when teaching elementary, junior high, and high school students. More creativity seems the norm and I'm happy to do more of it" (2009 NFWW survey participant).
- "Viewing the micro-teaching sessions and getting feedback from other faculty has encouraged me to take an experimental attitude towards teaching. I am now determined to try out different styles of presentation and evaluation" (2011 NFWW survey participant).

Step 2: Impact of Faculty Learning on Teaching

The next step in the chain from professional development to improved student learning is the application of learning to teaching. Experiences with students, as well as studies of professional development, suggest that this step is a difficult one. For example, Henderson, Dancy, and Niewiadomska-Bugaj (2012) report that even when faculty attempt to apply learning from professional development opportunities, it is not uncommon for them to fail to implement essential aspects of new pedagogy fundamental to transforming learning.

As described in chapter 3, the Tracer team, capitalizing on assignments collected as part of the portfolio analysis of student writing, sought to compare assignments developed before and after professional development experiences for individual faculty. This information was contextualized through interviews and in some cases observations of the faculty at work.

Evidence from Washington State University

At Washington State University, researchers were able to make use of a well-established tool for rating assignments that was aligned with the goals of the Critical Thinking Project professional development workshops. Fifty of the 350 faculty who had participated in the four-year Critical Thinking Project between 1999 and 2003 sat for interviews and provided samples of teaching materials from one of each subject's courses, focused in part on whether the critical thinking work was still an active part of faculty practice after seven to ten years.

In many ways, the Critical Thinking Project exemplified what is known about the very best in faculty development (Garet et al. 2001). It engaged participants over at least one year in several workshops; it provided data that described the results of faculty changes in practice; it engaged participants in presenting their work in colloquia or workshops within their own departments; it trained them as assessment raters (a very different role from grading); and the project as a whole addressed a concern shared universally among faculty: how to promote higher-order thinking in their students' course work. Finally, the project was grounded in a sound research design, so that students' improvements could be demonstrated to the faculty by data that the faculty could respect. Such an initiative ought to create substantial and continuing effects on teaching; interviews, syllabi, and assignments indicated that it had.

Faculty claimed in interviews—and their syllabi and materials confirmed it—that not only was promoting critical thinking still a goal in their teaching almost a decade later, but their practices had continued to evolve. In other words, the Project's goal of providing tools for continued innovation had been achieved. Not one of these faculty was using the same assignments, the same rubrics, or the same syllabus as the one(s) they reformed during the Project. Instead, there were several common features of their still-evolving practices:

- The practices they acquired during the Critical Thinking Project had migrated to all their courses, at all levels.
- Their materials—syllabi, assignments, grading practices—had continued to evolve.

- Faculty were using different, more sophisticated assignments, and they had revised their evaluative tools to reflect newer practices. In addition, they had used what they learned about promoting critical thinking to incorporate other learning outcomes, such as those detailed in WSU's Six Goals for the Baccalaureate, adopted two years after the end of the Critical Thinking Project.
- As faculty came across further ways of improving students' experiences, they readily incorporated them into their courses.
- Critical Thinking alumni attended significantly more faculty development events —1.3 more per semester—than their high-participating peers who had not participated in the original project. They also claimed that participation in the Project had changed for the better their opinions about faculty development events.
- Even after the Project had ended, these faculty were more likely than not (62 percent) to have presented a faculty development event within their own program or department or to have led an initiative to improve teaching in their department or program.

In all these cases, review of actual teaching materials confirmed faculty members' claims about changes.

Another fifty faculty members had participated in at least one two-day WAC workshop between 2000 and 2010, and their claims were similar to those from Critical Thinking participants, even though the experience of the WAC workshop is neither as intense nor as long in duration. Interviews and course materials again substantiated faculty members' claims about their teaching:

- Whatever the specific focus of the WAC workshop, participants continued to work on that aspect of their teaching over the ensuing years.
- Faculty could readily describe the evolution of an assignment or even a whole course over the years, and they could trace the influences of the WAC workshop they attended on those changes.
- Interviewees identified a wider range of effects from a WAC workshop than critical thinking participants did, indicating that continued learning takes the pathways established by the original learning event—the broader focus of the WAC workshops results in broader foci for faculty.
- WAC workshops were less empowering in one way: alumnae/i were less likely to have presented their work to colleagues or to have led a teaching initiative subsequent to the WAC workshop (only four had done so).
- Like their Critical Thinking counterparts, these faculty described teaching as a learning process, fed primarily by students' performances on course work—in other words, data driven.
- WAC workshop participants were less likely to say that their opinions about faculty development events had changed, but they universally agreed that they would participate in another WAC workshop (40 percent had already done so).

These data demonstrate the deep impact of the professional development program on faculty teaching. Not only did each faculty member revise one course or assignment (the direct goal of the workshop opportunities); they also applied their new learning broadly through their teaching and continued to evolve their teaching over time, thus demonstrating the large leveraging effect of professional development for faculty.

Data provided by WSU's Office of Institutional Research reveals that on average, across all types of appointment, faculty at WSU teach six courses per year. So what a teacher learns in order to improve one course spreads to six. In addition, the spread reaches from first-year or introductory courses to upper-division courses in the major to graduate seminars (Provost's Fact Book 2012). Finally, the longer the teacher stays on the faculty, the less likely that teacher will be teaching the same set of courses. In the sample pool of subjects at WSU, interviews revealed that faculty who had taught for six or more years since the initial workshop were infrequently still teaching more than one course that they had been teaching at the time of the workshop. Thus, faculty learning spreads its way across the curriculum. And since departments maintain files of syllabi and assignments as an aid to faculty who are teaching those courses for the first time, and because one of the most frequent vectors for spreading faculty learning is colleague-to-colleague (Beyer, Taylor, and Gillmore 2013), faculty learning has a number of ways of moving beyond the specific faculty learner. Investing in one faculty member's development has ripple effects that potentially reach an entire department or program, or even farther. In this way the resulting faculty learning can be conceptualized as distributed (Putnam and Borko 2000; Lave 1988) and no longer held by one individual faculty member. Two of the WSU subjects were members of WSU's Teaching Academy—faculty who are identified as excellent teachers and teaching resources for their colleagues. Their reach is university-wide.

Evidence for persistence in changes in teaching practices over time comes from both campuses. At Washington State University, where changes in administrative structure and the effects of the budget crises of the last half-decade have produced a changed landscape since the heyday of the Critical Thinking Project, the data are strong evidence for persistence and for continued development, even in the relative absence of formal development events. The Critical Thinking Project was a collaboration among the Center for Teaching, Learning, and Technology, the General Education Program, and the Campus Writing Programs. Today, as the result of the formation of a University College and drastic budget cuts, the first two of these programs no longer exist, and the expertise to run such an initiative was absent for seven years even from the Campus Writing Programs (the recent appointment of a new director has filled that vacuum as of January 2014). Conducting interviews and collecting assignments and syllabi from fifty former participants produced a long-term evaluation of the impact of the Critical Thinking Project, which ceased to operate in 2004. Clear evidence indicates that changes in teaching resulting from faculty development persist and grow over time. This finding was expected, given the rich learning pathways characterized by integration and application of knowledge identified in studying the impact of professional development on faculty at both WSU and Carleton.

Persistence was very clear in the faculty data sets at WSU, though the data show some differences in results that are dependent on the form of the original faculty development experience. The fifty faculty subjects who participated in the Critical Thinking Project (chosen out of 350 total participants) were still using techniques they had acquired seven to ten years earlier, when they participated in the project. All fifty had also exported their learning to other courses they teach, including both undergraduate and graduate courses.

Forty-seven demonstrated that they had continued to innovate. They used what they learned in the Project, but in the ensuing years they built on that foundation. For example, thirty-two faculty discussed how they used what they had learned about critical thinking to build one or more additional learning outcomes into their courses from the Six Learning Goals for the Baccalaureate. As their syllabi and assignments confirm, these faculty incorporated the learning outcomes, as appropriate, into a range of courses and in a range of manners. In a first-year art history course, this translated into providing students with three central sources for an argument about the Elgin Marbles controversy and asking students to find a fourth source for their essays. Upper-division and graduate course assignments included less scaffolding but pushed students to define their arguments more precisely (critical thinking) and to find better, more recent, more substantial sources to contextualize those arguments (information literacy) or to incorporate statistics as evidence (critical thinking, information literacy, and quantitative reasoning). Overall, these thirty-two faculty covered all six of the Six Outcomes for the Baccalaureate (derived from the Six Goals for the Baccalaureate) in their collective practices. In addition, they reported, and their syllabi and assignments confirmed, other common ways of extending their work in the project by further innovation:

- continuing to tweak assignments from the project based on feedback from students' performances (forty-one faculty)
- continuing to make course materials, including rubrics, challenge students to think critically (thirty-eight faculty)
- designing new assignments and materials for the original course, noting that their own evolving teaching practices demanded changes (thirty-four faculty)
- using established assignments as models for addressing similar learning outcomes in other courses (forty-six faculty)
- designing new courses at various levels, using knowledge about teaching critical thinking to make new courses more challenging and/or more appropriate to discipline, level, or students' abilities (thirty-six faculty)
- using teaching and grading experiences as data that indicate how they need to change their teaching practices (thirty-three faculty)

- refining their rubric practices to reduce time and/or uncertainty in the grading process (twenty-nine faculty)
- becoming comfortable sharing grading methods and criteria with students (thirty-four faculty)
- using information about grading criteria to introduce student peer review into their teaching practices (twenty-three faculty)
- coming to see teaching as an ever-evolving process, rather than as a static practice (forty-two faculty)
- feeling more comfortable taking risks (trying out new practices, new kinds of assignment, new content, etc.) in their teaching because their understanding of the process is stronger (thirty-three faculty)

All these developments serve as evidence of a faculty learning process that began in the Critical Thinking Project and was built into the faculty members' everyday practices in ways that allowed those practices to continue the evolution begun in the project. Only three faculty reported that they were simply using or adapting the same course materials, assignments, and rubrics they had designed years before. These three also indicated that their motivation for joining the project was the $1,000 stipend for completing it. Money is an important factor for getting faculty in the door, but these participants indicate that a stipend by itself does not produce the motivation for continued growth.

The fifty faculty who had attended at least one Writing Across the Curriculum (WAC) workshop claimed—and demonstrated in syllabi and assignments—outcomes that were a bit narrower and a bit less likely to produce continued innovation than was the case with the critical thinking participants.[1] WAC workshops, in contrast to the extensive and well-integrated activities of the Critical Thinking Project, are one-time, isolated events that serve an institutional purpose (in this case, supporting Writing in the Major courses) in a more ad hoc way. Since a two-day WAC workshop has been offered almost every year since 1987, a total of 1,123 faculty have attended at least one such workshop. However, since faculty who teach Writing in the Major ([M]) courses tend to be senior and since WSU has a high rate of faculty turnover, at the time the Tracer Project began only 143 faculty who had attended at least one WAC Workshop were still on staff.

Typically, twenty-five to thirty-five faculty participate in a given WAC workshop, the primary purpose of which is to support these faculty in integrating more writing into their courses, enabling the course to qualify as one of WSU's Writing in the Major [M] courses. Every student must complete at least two [M] courses, which are designed so that faculty in the student's major help the students learn to think and write as do practitioners in their major field (in the field, this is known as a "writing in the disciplines" model, or WID). While there is no fixed amount of writing required for these courses, writing must account for at least a third of the course grade, and students must be given opportunities early in the course to give and receive feedback on writing and to have opportunities to revise. A typical WAC workshop devotes one day to a guest expert (recent experts have included John Bean of Seattle University, Rebecca Moore Howard of Syracuse University, Helen Fox of the University of Michigan, and William Hart-Davidson of Michigan State University) and one day specifically focused on the goals of the [M] course. Faculty work in teams to support each other as they develop assignments and syllabi that will most closely promote the goals of the requirement. Given those goals (described above), the fifty faculty research participants most commonly listed (and their syllabi demonstrated) the following outcomes from the WAC workshop:

- learning how to address writing as a process, including multiple drafts, staged assignments, or cumulative assignments (forty-three faculty)
- scaffolding assignments so that students build competencies throughout the term (thirty-seven faculty)
- building disciplinary thinking more explicitly into writing assignments (forty-four faculty)
- engaging students in peer review as part of feedback (twenty-seven faculty)
- creating assignments that call on genres in use by practitioners in the field (thirty-four faculty)
- making evaluation of students' work more transparent (thirty-nine faculty)

These faculty were interviewed a minimum of one year after their participation, and the range was from one year (n=5) to 16 years (n=3), with the average time since the WAC workshop 6.2 years. Thus, these faculty compare well in this regard to those from the Critical Thinking Project. They achieved their goals for the workshop, and those outcomes persist into the present. In addition, most of these faculty (n=38) have exported their learning about building effective writing assignments to other courses that they teach. Of the thirty-eight who have done so, twenty-six also indicated that they have increased the amount of writing they assign in their other courses, ones that do not fulfill the Writing in the Major requirement. These faculty increased their comfort with assigning, responding to, and grading writing; thus, they were able to increase the overall amount of writing they assign—a win for the students and the curriculum.

A subset of twelve faculty had participated in at least two WAC workshops (including two who had attended three workshops, and one who had attended five), and they report adding several features to their practice. All twelve said that in their first experience, they had focused on what *they* came for—primarily help building better assignments and general knowledge about Writing in the Major [M] course expectations. But in that first workshop, their interest was piqued about additional possibilities that they did not yet feel ready to explore. These twelve repeat clients added the following practices or goals to their pedagogy:

- Nine were seeking ways to use rubrics or other methods of making their expectations and their standards clear to students.
- All twelve sought better ways of responding to student writing.
- Six wanted to follow up on ways of helping students identify and use better evidence in their papers.
- Four wanted to look at ways of giving students models of good writing without having those models become constraints on students' process of learning to write in the discipline.
- Nine wanted help building information literacy writing assignments.
- Ten wanted to use more ungraded writing as a tool for learning.

As was the case with the first-time outcomes, these practices, once introduced, persisted in the participants' course materials and were exported to the faculty's other courses as well. And some of the practices—rubrics, better response methods, providing models, in particular—helped these faculty increase the total amount of writing they assigned in a given semester, across all their courses.

Evidence from Carleton

At Carleton, interviews, surveys, and discourse analyses of faculty assignments indicate that faculty were implementing many of the practices that the WAC and QuIRK programming advocated. In eighteen of forty-seven interviews of those who had participated in professional development in the past, faculty described making changes to their teaching that aligned with WAC- or QuIRK-promoted pedagogies and mirrored the learning identified in post-workshop surveys. The dominant themes in the interviews included the following:

- encourage and assign multiple drafts as part of assignments
- utilize rubrics and/or clearly express expectations to students
- scaffold assignments to build up skills over the term
- help students to evaluate and use more numerate data
- encourage students to seek help from classroom instructors, peers, and staff on campus

Data from the 2010–2011 Higher Education Research Institute Survey at Carleton confirm this finding. One hundred thirty-eight of 234 faculty responded to this survey. Questions that are aligned with workshop goals received strong responses, indicating that faculty believe they are transferring this learning into their teaching (see table 4.1).

To move beyond self-report, Carleton researchers used a paired-comparison analysis of faculty assignments to evaluate the impact of professional development in these areas. Assignments were compared on eight items including guidelines for grading,

TABLE 4.1. COMPARISON OF 2010–2011 HIGHER EDUCATION RESEARCH INSTITUTE SURVEY (HERI) RESPONSES AT CARLETON COLLEGE AND GOALS OF CARLETON TEACHING INITIATIVES

WAC AND QUIRK TEACHING INITIATIVES HAVE EMPHASIZED:	HERI SURVEY DATA
Critical thinking in the process of learning, writing, and analyzing scholarly work	96.4% of Carleton respondents reported that it was essential to teach critical thinking
Evaluating and using data, research material, and secondary sources	68.8% of the survey respondents also reported that it was essential to help students evaluate the quality and reliability of information (another 27.5% reported that this was very important)
Encouraging students to seek help, peer review, and timely responses to student work	81.8% reported that they frequently encouraged students to seek feedback on their academic work
Including drafts in assignments	59.4% reported that they frequently ask students to revise their papers (another 30.4% reported that they did this occasionally)

use of data, articulation of learning goals, and inclusion of drafts in assignments. Findings showed that high-participating faculty generally produced assignments rated "better" according to the faculty development goals. In particular, the newer assignments from those high-participating faculty cued students to support writing with evidence, including data, and the assignments described learning goals, grading standards, and other specifics in more detail.

Tracer researchers at Carleton learned more about the interactions between multiple faculty development activities through an ethnographic study of five instructors who were teaching freshmen seminars at Carleton in the fall term of 2010. These faculty members volunteered to allow observation of their courses, participate in interviews, and permit collection of copies of their assignment prompts, syllabi, and students' writing (with students' informed consent). The five faculty members' teaching trajectories were typical of many Carleton faculty members' iterative movements between learning about teaching and teaching innovation. The following description of a case study instructor illustrates this general pathway from faculty development to teaching and learning at Carleton, as a new faculty member soaks up everything she can about teaching in the beginning of her career and then becomes more particular about her faculty development interests as she develops her teaching over time.

Associate professor Samantha Hogan (not her real name) arrived at Carleton in the fall of 2002 with limited teaching experience as a graduate teaching assistant and in a one-year teaching position at a small liberal arts college. Professor Hogan's only teacher training prior to Carleton was a short observation/discussion of her teaching in graduate school and a workshop on public speaking that she attended at the liberal arts college. Acknowledging the need to learn much more about teaching when she arrived at Carleton, she jumped at the chance to attend WAC workshops. She described the most effective part of WAC workshops and portfolio rating sessions as the opportunity to see and learn from other faculty members' assignments and their students' writing. Furthermore, in the workshops, she valued the chance to design assignments of her own and to get other faculty members' feedback on them. Overall, Professor Hogan noted that faculty development participation makes sense for any faculty member—new or seasoned—because

> professors, they love being in school. That's the reason they're professors, right? And so it's another opportunity to learn and to hear about something new, and how to do something better that we're already doing. (interview, Winter 2010)

Like other faculty members at Carleton, Professor Hogan's interest in improving her teaching—and learning in general—through faculty development coincided with an interest in participating in any campus activity that would enable her to learn more about Carleton's culture and to meet new people.

From 2002 to 2007, Professor Hogan participated in eight WAC activities, including four workshops, a curriculum development grant from WAC, two portfolio rating sessions (one was required as part of her grant and one was voluntary), and a book group. She was particularly active in faculty development in her first two years, participating in six activities between December 2002 and late August of 2004. Professor Hogan describes several important ways that her assignments and teaching benefited from her WAC participation. She began scaffolding writing into her courses and encouraging students to write more drafts. Furthermore, she changed how she discussed writing with her students with an expanded vocabulary about writing. Finally, she changed how she evaluated students' writing by using a rubric (which she provides to the students) and by commenting on digital copies of students' work. This digital commenting system and rubric allows her to give students feedback on their writing much more quickly than she had in the past. This increased turnaround in feedback provides her students with more time to revise their work and take her comments into consideration in time to apply this information to further assignments in the course.

From 2007 to 2008, Professor Hogan's faculty development participation evolved along with corresponding changes in faculty development offerings at the college and her own different learning needs at a more advanced stage in her career. She participated in a mixture of WAC and QuIRK activities, including sophomore portfolio ratings (Summer 2009 and 2010), and a joint WAC/QuIRK winter workshop in 2010; and she is now one of the QuIRK program leaders on campus. Although she earned tenure and has become more comfortable in her teaching, she continues to participate in forms of faculty development and to revise her courses and assignments—though as her expertise increases, these revisions are less drastic than they were earlier in her career. Now, she fine-tunes the ways that she teaches writing, and particularly writing with numbers. For example, she makes sure that she gives students opportunities to practice writing with numbers because, for younger students,

> I think that intellectually they understand what a bad argument looks like or what a bad argument with numbers looks like, and they can recognize it when they see it. But then being able to then produce it themselves, and recognize it after they've produced it, is very hard for them. (interview, Winter 2010)

In the fall of 2010, eight sessions of Professor Hogan's freshman seminar were observed and interviews were conducted with her before and after the course. Her students' writing and her assignment prompts were analyzed with WSU's Critical Thinking Rubric and the Carleton faculty-development influenced rubric. Using the paired-comparison method of analysis described earlier, faculty raters evaluated Professor Hogan's newer assignment as better than her older assignment in relation to enlisting faculty development-promoted pedagogies. The newer assignment provided students with clear guidelines, required them to exercise higher-order thinking, required them to use appropriate data/evidence to support their arguments, and provided students with opportunities for feedback. The participant observations and analyses documented Professor Hogan performing fifteen of the twenty-one WAC- and QuIRK-supported practices that were coded across interviews, surveys, faculty assignment prompts, and case study observations. The scaffolding that she described in interviews took the form of smaller papers that helped students practice their writing with quick feedback and revisions before turning their attention to a larger writing assignment. Professor Hogan leveraged the help of reference librarians and academic technicians to instruct the students in the logistics and rationale for using technology to construct compelling and data-rich pieces of writing. She could then spend more time guiding the students' learning through discussion of the course material (in class and online) and to help the students take ownership of their own learning. She enlisted peer review and group work projects as part of this endeavor.

This case study of Professor Hogan illustrates the ways that faculty development can affect teaching practices in very concrete, as well as abstract, ways. Professor Hogan attended different kinds of faculty development over time, depending both on the college's faculty development offerings and on her own changing needs as she developed her teaching. She introduced new types of assignments and approaches to teaching when they aligned with her own courses' learning goals and her need for better efficiency and feedback for students. Professor Hogan took practices she learned in WAC workshops and portfolio rating sessions—such as the use of grading rubrics and scaffolding assignments—and put them into practice in most of her courses. In addition, she developed a positive attitude toward learning about teaching and getting help for teaching, and she observed better learning on the part of her students as a result of these changes, which reinforced her interest in continuing to learn about teaching and learning (albeit in more targeted ways as she advanced in her career).

Summary of Evidence from Both Institutions

In sum, at both Carleton College and Washington State University, faculty participating in professional development activities learn new teaching techniques and apply them broadly in their teaching. The workshop programs, which reflect effective teaching practices themselves, are producing the desired effects, and changes are making their way into participants' assignments, both the assignments that were the focus of study at the workshop and beyond. These improvements persist in faculty teaching and are recognizable in assignments developed long after the end of the workshop. There is indeed a recognizable impact of faculty development on teaching.

However, at both Carleton and WSU, the research process led to the conclusion that the single workshop is not the correct unit of measure. The ethnographic and interview data clearly show the interaction of multiple workshops over time. It is no more fruitful to try to isolate the impact of a single workshop from the cumulative learning experiences of a faculty member than it is to try to understand the impact of a single course on the learning of an undergraduate student. When teaching is successful and learning is occurring, the learner integrates knowledge and experience from the past with new information and applies it widely and over time. At both WSU and Carleton, faculty participate in opportunities of different types, building their skills and knowledge while changing their attitudes and beliefs.

An Alternative Path: Impact of Portfolio Rating on Teaching

Routine events in the management of a campus can provide strong opportunities for faculty professional development and learning. Both WSU and Carleton College engage substantial numbers of faculty in assessing a mid-career writing portfolio from every student (table 4.2).

This project identified portfolio rating as a site where faculty might observe student work in ways that contribute to improving faculty members' pedagogy. While carefully analyzing samples of student writing for the purpose of assessment or research, faculty and staff on both campuses report learning the following:

- the kinds of writing that they can expect from students by the end of their second year in college
- the wide range of writing genres that faculty are requiring freshmen and sophomore students to learn in their classes across the curriculum
- ways that other faculty members write assignments in their courses and the kinds of writing that result from these assignment prompts (in part)

**TABLE 4.2. COMPARATIVE DATA ON PORTFOLIO RATING
AT WASHINGTON STATE AND CARLETON**

	WSU	CARLETON
Number of Portfolios per Academic Year	4,500	450
Number of Faculty Raters Trained	350	140
Number Required for One Year's Rating	Approximately 50	35
Rating Sessions Held	Approximately 50, as needed throughout the year	1, in June
% Raters from Departments Other than English	82	88

- other faculty raters' ideas about effective pedagogy, curricular expectations, and student writing in general (see also Rutz and Lauer-Glebov 2005, 90)
- the kinds of writing in which students genuinely invest, versus the kinds that inspire only compliance with the assignment
- the variations in genre, style, voice, content, and evidence among the disciplines
- the standards to which faculty across the institution hold students with regard to performance in writing

At WSU, interviews with forty raters, combined with analysis of their writing assignments, yielded a wealth of information about portfolio rating as an agent of faculty learning. While gains often depend on faculty motivation for rating (i.e., those participating primarily for the money tend to learn less), most faculty experience a range of perceptions and feelings during rating. They are alternately impressed about and dismayed over the respectively high or low standards their colleagues enforce. They see a wide range of tools for evaluating students' writing. They see exciting writing and boring writing, and they often revise their own assignments to reflect strategies that provoke exciting writing from students. Every rater could point to significant changes in his or her construction of writing assignments as a result of lessons learned from reading so much student writing, so many student texts.[2]

Beyond the direct experience of rating portfolios, rating has led to a type of norming for faculty teaching, especially among younger faculty at both institutions. The socialization about teaching through these sessions shapes and legitimizes the teaching knowledge and norms for the campus community (Webster-Wright 2009) and contributes to the effective culture of teaching and learning. Rating has also provided inspiration for interdisciplinary teaching or research projects, especially at WSU, where contact with faculty outside one's own department is not as common as it is at Carleton. The results of such contacts at WSU can be seen in dyad courses taught by faculty from very different disciplines (e.g., geology and history, English and architecture, rhetoric and horticulture) and at Carleton in collaborations among staff and faculty on particular courses (e.g., help from the Writing Program Director in designing an assignment for a biology course). Moreover, raters are automatically exposed to the full range of resources available from the writing program: workshops, consultations, writing tutorials, research literature, and so forth. In addition to acting itself as a powerful site of faculty development, rating serves as a pipeline to other, more formal development opportunities.

The two cases below, one drawn from each institution, illustrate the ways in which portfolio rating produces new understanding which is then integrated into ongoing learning and changes in teaching. They also illuminate the important social context that can emerge from professional development that is part of the routine operations of the institution.

Carleton Rater

> There is a real sense, I think, of collegiality on this campus. And I know if it weren't for those sources of (faculty development) events, I would only talk to people in my department. (tenure-track faculty, Carleton)

This assistant professor had just returned from participating in a sophomore student writing portfolio rating session in which he helped a wide cross-section of faculty and staff to identify students who were in need of some extra writing help, as well as those who could be commended for their excellent writing. His office was deep in an older building in one of Carleton's larger departments (fifteen instructional faculty), and it made sense that he could easily find himself isolated there with just his departmental colleagues and students. The professor explained that he had often sought out workshops in order to obtain direct help for developing an assignment as well as a general interest in becoming a better professor (especially early in his career at the school). Beyond the individual workshop topics, the experiences often provided him with an opportunity to meet and obtain help from colleagues across the campus after the workshop ended. For example, in one particular workshop about teaching with visual material, he described how "the conversations I had with other participants were very, very helpful and making connections with people who I could later go back and talk to and begin to develop my assignment." He believed that the assignment he designed with staff and colleague help was quite successful.

WSU Rater

> I like rating portfolios because it's one of the few times when I get to sit down and interact with colleagues from other departments, especially in a semi-serious, semi-

social way. We talk a lot about what we're seeing in the portfolios and how that compares with what we see in our own students. I've learned so much about writing in other fields—especially fields like Business or Agriculture or Engineering that are so different from my own. And about teaching practices in those places. I like the pay, but at this point I'd almost rate portfolios for free. The sessions are that valuable to me.

This associate professor from the College of Liberal Arts was invited to train as a rater by virtue of her teaching a Writing in the Major course in her department. She was in her third year of rating and participated often: more than ten sessions per year. Her department of thirty-two tenure-track faculty, forty-six full-time instructors, and an assortment of part-time adjuncts is one of the largest on campus, and in that situation she said that she had to make strong efforts to reach outside her department for conversations with colleagues. She likes her department and finds her colleagues friendly; however, she feels isolated from the rest of the faculty on a day-to-day basis, since her interactions tend to stay within her department. Since 82 percent of portfolio raters are from departments other than English, this rater came to see rating sessions as her gateway to the rest of the university. She claimed to talk more about teaching with fellow raters than with departmental colleagues. And she could point to the rating sessions as the source for specific changes she had made in her approach to teaching and in particular course assignments.

Participation in portfolio review at both campuses serves as a second model for faculty development. In this case the design of the professional activity focuses on studying the relationship between assignment design and student learning. Faculty leave with new norms and expectations for both their assignments and students' work. At Carleton, where portfolio rating is designed to incorporate formal faculty development and where faculty raters routinely participate in a wide range of formal and routine development opportunities, separating the effects of portfolio rating from the various effects from other faculty learning opportunities is frankly impossible. However, the WSU rater corps included some raters who had not participated in either the Critical Thinking Project or in any WAC workshops. Therefore, the fact that they reported changes that resulted from their rating experiences—changes that were confirmed in their syllabi and assignments—provides strong evidence for the effect of such a routine activity on a participant's teaching.

Low-Participating Faculty

The preceding sections have described the profound effect of professional development on faculty who participate extensively. A primary finding of this work is that the number of faculty participating fully was much larger than anticipated and it proved extremely difficult to find faculty who had participated in absolutely no form of faculty development. However, it would be misleading to suggest that the cases above are typical of all faculty. Engagement of faculty can be described as a spectrum from fully engaged to low-participating faculty. The impact on low participators is perceivable though substantially less than on high participators.

At WSU, interviews with twenty-eight low-participating faculty (those reporting fewer than three development events per year of any kind) confirmed that the sites of faculty learning at more routine events occur as a result of a wide variety of functions faculty members serve that are not directly related to teaching. At both WSU and Carleton, conversations about accreditation were often mentioned as a source of faculty learning, even among faculty who did not seek help with their teaching.

When asked, low-participating faculty identified such activities as the source for various changes in their teaching practices. The twenty-eight WSU participants could all point to at least one significant change that came out of departmental events. All cited at least one formal event per year, usually a departmental colloquium or other meeting that focused on teaching, curriculum, outcomes, and so on. Most also cited at least one more routine event. As a result of these events, low-participating faculty (serving as a comparison group)

- added to or altered existing course outcomes
- changed their expectations for students' work—in all but one case, toward higher standards
- adopted a new method for evaluating student work
- developed a new assignment or significantly revised an existing one
- consulted with a colleague who is regarded as an accomplished teacher

All twenty-eight reported making changes, and all twenty-eight could account for some means of evaluating the effect of those changes. Their statements were verified by assignment analysis. In short, though they were not aware of doing so, they were working on their teaching effectiveness, though in smaller increments and at a slower pace than their high-participating colleagues.

Interviews at Carleton showed similar changes in low participators' teaching— whether conscious or not. Professor Perkins, a mid-career faculty member in a social science department, at first told a researcher that his main "faculty development" was the self-directed reading he does at the beginning of the summer. Later in the interview, however, he described making changes related to quantitative reasoning in a course that he co-taught with a younger faculty member. He had been impressed by her teaching and by other young faculty members that he had observed while participating in their third-year and tenure evaluations. His co-instructor (and perhaps the other younger faculty as well) was highly involved in QuIRK and she certainly could have influenced his subsequent decision to apply for a curriculum development grant from this same program.

Thanks to the scarcity of low-participating faculty, only a single analysis of paired assignments from such a faculty member was completed at Carleton. Using the comparison method for assignment analysis, two faculty raters decided that this faculty member's newer assignment was "somewhat better" than his older assignment in eliciting higher-order thinking. One rater thought that the newer assignment was better at providing students with "guidelines for grading that are clearly articulated (and include writing standards)," and the other rater thought that the newer assignment was better at requiring students to use data/evidence or quantitative reasoning. Nonetheless, his newer assignment was not as well aligned to faculty development elements as some of the other, higher-participating faculty members' newer assignments. This single sample is suggestive in that it confirms the inferences drawn from a wider sample of interviews. A stronger conclusion would require a larger analysis.

On each campus, select faculty members remained less enthusiastic about participating in formal activities of faculty development (or voluntary routine events that have incidental faculty learning opportunities) and were not always as eager to experiment in their teaching. These faculty might learn some of the higher participators' pedagogy and approaches through conversations with their colleagues in hallways, faculty development events in their departments, or in department reviews; but they were still less interested in actively pursuing knowledge about teaching than these other colleagues. Low participators' attitudes demonstrate the continued need for improving views about teaching in particular disciplines, departments, and institutional structures, environments, and reward systems.

Looking More Broadly: Effect of Campus Culture on Impact of Professional Development on Teaching

One of the principal findings of the study is that more faculty are participating in faculty development, intentionally or not, than had been predicted. Much has been written about institutional barriers to improvements in teaching (Sabagh and Saroyan 2014). The central theme that emerged on both campuses is that substantial numbers of faculty seek out development activities because teachers care deeply about their teaching. Even in the absence of a central agency for formal faculty development (i.e., WSU's abolition of its Center for Teaching, Learning, and Technology), faculty sought out venues for formal development and continued to innovate. End of workshop surveys for faculty development events (2009 and 2010) at Carleton College reveal that nearly two-thirds of participants (131 out of 216) were motivated to attend the workshop because of either a specific quandary they wanted to address in their teaching and/ or general pedagogical interest. Faculty at both institutions engage in faculty development, as both participants and leaders in these activities, and as leaders they set priorities for development initiatives and plan and carry out those initiatives (robust examples include WSU's Critical Thinking Project, WSU's and Carleton's Writing Portfolios, and Carleton's QuIRK Project).

Despite high demands on their time (including research, campus service, and personal demands), faculty still devote a substantial amount of time and effort to improving their teaching, and that time and effort bears fruit in actual, substantial changes. Through multiple sites of faculty learning, faculty in this study learned pedagogy and content that they could immediately implement in their teaching, as demonstrated in data from faculty members' responses to various activities and case studies from Carleton College that show an individual's pathway from faculty development to teaching innovation. These data confirm research in SoTL that demonstrates marked effects of faculty development on teachers' practices—on the ways they construct their courses, the activities they use to engage students in class and on assignments, and on the ways they evaluate students' work (Huber 2006; Weimer 2006). Faculty see teaching as engaging in a process of continual learning and improvement.

Differences in Impact Resulting from Faculty Status

One of the most surprising discoveries about the impact of faculty development on teaching practices was the degree to which faculty status impinged on progress.

At WSU, where 41 percent of classes are taught by adjuncts, fifty-six of the one hundred sixty-eight faculty interviewed were either part-time adjuncts (sixteen) or on full-time, temporary appointments (forty). While these faculty held positions in a wide range of departments (in the sciences, humanities, arts, and applied sciences), a significant number—twelve—came from General Education's World Civilizations course (a two-semester, universal requirement for first-year students, which has since been discontinued as the result of General Education reform) and the next largest contingent—ten—taught in the English department's Composition Program. Overall, the fifty-six temporary faculty taught a wide range of courses, centered in the lower division, but also including upper-division courses in technical writing, digital technology and culture, art history, kinesiology, electrical engineering, and education, as well as professional-school clinical teaching in veterinary medicine, pharmacy, and agricultural research.

In every case at WSU, temporary faculty participated more frequently in both formal faculty development and routine events that produced incidental faculty learning about teaching. Nine were writing portfolio raters, for example. None of WSU's comparison group of low-participating faculty had non-tenure track appointments. The twenty-two temporary faculty in World Civilizations and the Composition Program reported by far the highest rate of participation in formal faculty development, and most of their events were sponsored or directly offered by the programs in which they taught. Still, more than 90 percent of temporary faculty sought out both formal faculty development activities and routine events beyond those offered in their home departments or programs.

TABLE 4.3. TEMPORARY FACULTY'S ATTENDANCE AT
FORMAL FACULTY DEVELOPMENT EVENTS

HOME/ DEPARTMENT PROGRAM	NO. OF PARTICIPANTS (N=56)	AVERAGE NO. OF EVENTS PER YEAR	AVERAGE OFFERED BY HOME DEPARTMENT/ PROGRAM	AVERAGE OUTSIDE HOME DEPARTMENT/ PROGRAM
World Civ	12	12	10	2
Composition	10	23	18	5
Music	4	7	3	4
Education	3	8	5	3
Engineering	2	11	9	2
Vet Med	4	13	11	2
Pharmacy	2	9	5	4
Digital Technology and Culture	3	18	16	2
Art History	2	9	4	5
Agriculture	2	11	9	2
Kinesiology	3	9	6	3
Other	9	8	5	3
Average		**11.5**	**8.4**	**3.1**

Table 4.3 details the average number of formal faculty development events attended by temporary faculty in the various departments or programs in a single academic year. A few programs and departments offered a very high number of events because those units use a much higher number of temporary faculty than others do. Those programs tend also to offer a high number of formal events (see, for example, the averages for World Civilizations and Composition). Departments with fewer temporary faculty tend to offer fewer events, and those faculty sought out more events held outside their home departments or programs.

As interviews with these faculty proceeded, some surprising similarities developed between temporary and tenure-line faculty. All had terminal degrees, and all but a few had PhDs. Temporary faculty resembled tenure-stream faculty in terms of length of service, too. Since the project interviewed faculty who had been on campus at least long enough to attend a WAC Workshop, subjects' length of service ranged from two years to a high of twenty-seven. The longest-serving participant, with twenty-seven years' service, was among the temporary faculty. On average, the temporary faculty had served 8.5 years, most having taught in several departments or programs along the way in order to maintain full-time or nearly full-time employment.

Tenure-stream participants averaged 9.4 years' service, though most had taught in only one department or program during that time. Given the heavier teaching loads for temporary faculty (full time is four courses per semester, as opposed to two courses per semester for tenure-track faculty), temporary faculty were actually far more experienced teachers than their tenure-line colleagues. In short, there is no discernible reason to suspect that these teachers' responses to faculty development would differ sharply, though the greater participation by temporary faculty, along with their greater teaching experience, could lead to the inference that temporary faculty might be more innovative, resourceful teachers. However, the reverse turned out to be true, leading to some further comparisons between temporary faculty and tenure-track faculty, comparisons that have implications for higher education staffing as a whole.

First, while teachers in both categories seek out opportunities to improve their teaching, their motives differ starkly. Tenure-line faculty, even high-participating individuals, participate in far fewer events than do temporary faculty. High-participating tenure-track faculty reported attending an average of 5.1 events per year, taking formal and other routine activities together, while table 4.3 shows that, on average, temporary faculty attended 8.4 formal faculty development events per year. Temporary faculty reported that they practiced "defensive" faculty development. These teachers sought to improve their teaching, but they also "showed the flag" at development events, both within and outside their home programs, since attendance reflected well on their future employability. They uniformly claimed that they needed to demonstrate their dedication to teaching by attending these events. In addition to building their teaching practice, they needed to be seen at these events. Kezar and Eckel (2002) found that this defensive stance and fear of being perceived as behind others was a motivator for involvement in campus change initiatives. Fear of losing one's non-tenure-track position for even a slight faltering in teaching excellence can be characteristic of research institutions. Kezar and Eckel showed that this behavior was well aligned with both the collegial culture described by Bergquist (1992) and the socialization processes put forward by Tierney (1997). Results from interviews with WSU non-tenure-track faculty confirm that this culture of defensive faculty development is widespread in higher education.

Similar behavior occurred at Carleton among newer tenure-track faculty, who also wanted to demonstrate their interest in improving teaching, as well as to use faculty development opportunities as a means for networking among senior scholars who might serve on their tenure and promotion committees. In contrast, no WSU tenure-line faculty member claimed a need to be seen at these events, nor any possible advantage other than improving teaching. The inference: the motivation of new faculty at Carleton and of non-tenure line faculty at WSU reflects a culture that emphasizes improvements in teaching. This motivation was not present for tenure-line faculty at WSU; their motivation was entirely personal.

Second, and ironically, the rate of innovation differs in exactly the opposite way one might expect, given the numbers above. Tenure-line faculty reported that they experimented widely with any new methods or assignments or technologies that appealed to them. Tenure-track WAC workshop participants immediately tried out in class the assignments or techniques they learned about in the workshops, keeping what worked and discarding what either didn't work for them or wasn't worth the effort. These faculty attended development opportunities in order to innovate in their own classrooms. Since they were on the tenure track, they did not have a great fear about consequences of innovation, namely, lower evaluations and seeming to stumble in the classroom—in short, failure of one kind or another. Similarly, Carleton's newer, tenure-track faculty were eager to demonstrate to senior faculty that they were experimenting in their teaching. However, it is worth noting that at least four outlier interviewees reported being concerned about receiving potentially low evaluations based on too much experimentation. Although this concern did not in fact keep them from experimenting, two of these interviewees explained that their worries about student evaluations were compounded by concern that students evaluated them more harshly than their male and/or white counterparts.

Temporary faculty at WSU, by contrast, rarely reported trying out new assignments or practices immediately, unless they could see straightaway that the new methods were already clearly working well for other colleagues. Most of these faculty were on one-year, full-time appointments, while a few were teaching on one-semester, part-time loads—and all were hired to *teach*. Their reappointments depended totally on effective teaching, *as measured by student course evaluations;* in fact, almost all reported that the message in their programs was that the best teachers stayed and the rest could be replaced. That message is likely similar to what temporary faculty hear nationally: success is measured in terms of teaching evaluations, so keep them high or risk not being reappointed. Therefore, at WSU temporary faculty became more cautious about innovation. They are slower to adopt new methods, and their assignments demonstrate that they are also slower to make changes that reflect their faculty development experience. Among WAC Workshop participants, for example, temporary faculty reported that they maintained contact with tenure-stream colleagues so that they could see how new ideas worked out. Once temporary faculty could see (1) that a new technique was working in an actual classroom and (2) *why* it was successful, then and only then would they introduce it into their own classrooms.

Finally, the greater willingness to innovate resulted in higher performance for students in courses taught by tenure-track faculty (see table 4.4). Yes, these faculty sometimes saw student course evaluations dip when the teachers tried something really new, but the payoff for experimentation was greater learning. Tenure-line faculty, thus, became the innovators, the pioneers and early adopters of newer, more effective methods, tools, and assignments—because only 40 percent of their performance reviews address teaching, and because employment security granted them license to try new

TABLE 4.4. AVERAGE WASHINGTON STATE UNIVERSITY
CRITICAL THINKING (CT) RATINGS BY APPOINTMENT TYPE

	ADJUNCT (TERM-TO-TERM)	TEMPORARY (YEAR-TO-YEAR)	TENURE-TRACK
Average CT score for assignments	3.7	3.9	4.3
Average CT score for students' work samples	3.4	4.1	4.4

things. Temporary faculty, who were equally qualified and more experienced in the classroom, proved to be effective teachers, but their students lagged a bit behind students of tenure-stream faculty, most likely because the temporary faculty members stuck to well-established, proven methods, tools, and assignments.

At Carleton, there are few adjunct faculty. The important difference in status is between permanent, tenure-line faculty and temporary or visiting faculty. Interview participants included two visiting scholars at Carleton who were outliers in relation to the other visiting professors. Both of these individuals were still working on their PhDs and were teaching on one-year contracts. Carleton frequently hires such individuals to fill vacancies caused by sabbatical or other leaves of absence. These two faculty were reluctant to attend many faculty development activities and, in one case, to experiment with new pedagogies unless specifically advised by senior scholars in the department to incorporate a particular assignment or approach. Both faculty were extremely pressed for time due to the pressures of finishing their dissertations, finding employment, family concerns, and planning for moves.

Nevertheless, all visiting faculty members at Carleton, including the two outliers, are enculturated along with other new faculty at the college. They attend the same New Faculty Orientation in the fall and are invited to participate in the New Faculty Winter Workshop after their first term at Carleton, during which they are all encouraged to innovate and experiment in their teaching. No participant in these workshops from either group voiced concern about experimenting with new pedagogies, either in person or in post-workshop evaluation surveys.

Regular faculty and visitors contracted for at least two academic years also have the same opportunities for obtaining internal grants for curriculum development and research development (including developing and leading off-campus study programs). They are expected to participate in departmental and college faculty meetings and activities and they can take advantage of campus amenities such as low-cost housing, recreation facilities, and food discounts.

However, there are certainly added challenges for visiting faculty members at Carleton. Visitors do not receive the same amount of college funding as tenured/

tenure-track faculty for disciplinary conferences and faculty development outside of the college. Furthermore, as shown by the two outliers above, they must still spend significant amounts of time searching for future employment elsewhere, in addition to their full- or part-time teaching duties. Nonetheless—even with these added employment, time, and financial stresses—visiting faculty attended faculty development opportunities during the academic term in equal numbers to regular faculty. For example, they attended Perlman Center for Learning and Teaching (LTC) activities in almost equal percentages with regular faculty. In 2010, twenty-one of a possible thirty-five visiting faculty attended LTC events (60 percent), at the same time that 144 of a possible 225 regular faculty and lecturers attended LTC events (64 percent).

These activities occur at lunchtime, include meals, and—as described above—provide opportunities for networking. Visiting faculty learn more about teaching while meeting other faculty who may be able to help them pursue an academic career (as was similarly the case with Professor Hogan and other new faculty). In an interview, Professor Wilson, a visiting assistant professor, said that she was partially motivated to attend faculty development activities in order to make "contacts on campus,"

> and that's invaluable because then I'll see somebody else, I mean, someone somewhere else, and then we'll have a conversation about what we learned, or we'll see each other at another conference, or another workshop, and then we'll remember, you know, this is how we can link that to that.

At the time of the interview, this younger scholar was designing a new course with assignments inspired by one faculty development program and taking advantage of research and teaching help from a variety of other faculty within and beyond her department on campus.

Interview and observation material also suggested that the tenuous nature of visiting faculty members' employment at Carleton did not appear to influence their interest in experimenting with new pedagogies in their teaching any more than it did for regular faculty. Professor Wilson also described in glowing terms how other faculty encouraged her to make use of Carleton resources and to develop her teaching and research projects:

> I think I did come on campus with ideas, because I've been fermenting them for four years. . . . But where I did get to do some things (before Carleton), I put a few projects together and wrote some grants, but that's when I realized there was a lack of funds and a lack of support. So when I arrived here with the same ideas, everyone that I talked to was excited or showed enthusiasm, and then other people said talk to so and so, they may have funds for you. So I couldn't understand why I wouldn't do anything.

Thus, it appears that at Carleton, in contrast to the situation at WSU, visiting or temporary faculty behave very similarly to tenure-line faculty. They attend the same number of events during the academic year, differing only in their use of events taking place during breaks. Both groups seek and obtain funds for developing and revising courses, and all call on their colleagues for help. Perhaps most importantly, both groups experiment in their courses without fear. Visiting faculty understand that tenure-line faculty can assist them as their careers move forward.

These differences show profoundly the impact of campus culture on classroom innovation and improvement. At Carleton, all faculty, including visiting or temporary faculty, are engaged in improving their teaching as part of a campus culture that promotes and values such innovation. At WSU, a large group of adjunct faculty understand that the university values their teaching ability, so they seek to demonstrate their continual engagement in improvement. However, these faculty do not feel that they can innovate safely and thus require more than knowledge of improved pedagogies to transform their teaching.

Faculty Development Impacts Teaching

On both campuses, strong evidence exists that learning about teaching leads to improved teaching. Again and again, on both campuses, faculty could identify multiple, specific changes they had made in their course content, pedagogy, syllabi, and assignments; and faculty could tie those changes to specific events or resources available on their campuses. Faculty who are participating fully in opportunities to enhance their teaching have stronger teaching assignments as measured objectively by independent raters. When asked, these faculty tell a rich story of personal motivation, professional motivation, campus culture, and student results that impel them forward to learning more about teaching and learning. Faculty at Carleton and at WSU followed similar trajectories in their development as teachers: iterative pathways from learning about teaching, to teaching innovations, to more learning about teaching. While faculty who participate at low levels in faculty development show evidence of campus-based priorities creeping into their assignments, high-participating faculty capitalizing on professional development opportunities outperform low-participating faculty. Further, as demonstrated by the comparison between tenure-line and other faculty, the institutional context can promote or hinder both learning and application of that knowledge. When the institution expresses its values about teaching by providing a rich set of opportunities for the faculty learning part of the cycle and by building rewards for better student learning into faculty evaluation cycles, the most powerful results will occur.

Interviews on both campuses revealed the importance of routine campus events like portfolio assessment and preparing for accreditation review in fostering faculty learning. Any occasion for faculty to engage in meaningful discussions of teaching supports learning and motivates improvements in teaching. Portfolio rating which engages large numbers of faculty in reading and discussing students' responses to course assignments has played a particularly profound role at both WSU and Carleton.

This socialization of the learning through discourse shapes the professional pathways of these faculty and legitimizes this teaching knowledge, particularly for temporary, non-tenure-line and new faculty who rely on norming their teaching practice to others at the institution.

Findings from temporary faculty at WSU provide a cautionary tale demonstrating ways in which context can impede improvement. Temporary faculty depend on their colleagues heavily for reasons that go beyond improving teaching and that have everything to do with their future employment. These dependencies play out very differently at Carleton and WSU. At WSU, the data show that these faculty are in almost every way the equals of their tenure-track colleagues, and that the constraints on innovation result from institutional processes—from their status as temporary employees and their vulnerability to low student evaluations—rather than from any difference in ability or desire. At WSU these faculty teach more courses with larger enrollment than do tenure-track faculty, indicating the importance of this finding. At Carleton, a strong culture is supportive of innovation for all faculty. Temporary faculty seeking strong faculty recommendations are thus motivated to innovate.

Uniformly, faculty at Carleton and at WSU implemented what they learned about teaching into their course plans and continued to innovate on their own as they evaluated the work students did in response to course assignments and other activities. (For temporary faculty at WSU, these changes were predicated on more than knowledge gained at the professional development activity itself requiring verification of successful implementation by tenure-line faculty.) When the momentum of these changes began to slow, faculty returned for further learning or sought other forms of input to continue their improvement as teachers, which they measured, informally, by the improvements in their students' performances.

Tracing the first steps from professional development to changes in teaching leads to the conclusion that there is strong evidence of large impact. At both Carleton and WSU, faculty are choosing to participate in well-designed, faculty-driven development efforts, and they are learning from these activities as well as from routine events like promotion and tenure reviews, program evaluation, or portfolio rating. Colleges or universities wondering whether faculty development is a good investment can take heart that these efforts result in substantial changes in teaching across a campus. Clearly, funding devoted to faculty development bears fruit in improved teaching.

5 Spreading the Benefits

Tʀᴀᴄᴇʀ Pʀᴏᴊᴇᴄᴛ ᴅᴀᴛᴀ show that when an individual faculty member applies his or her learning to revise existing assignments or develop new ones, or to revise an existing course or develop a new one, he or she initiates a chain of improvements in teaching that amplify and spread the impact of professional development opportunities. When faculty members successfully apply their learning to the courses or assignments that were the focus of the faculty development opportunity, they routinely apply that learning to the rest of their courses and assignments. These two extensions of the faculty development reveal the most basic spread of effect. Another important avenue for spread of effect is the question of how some faculty members' learning might spread to colleagues or throughout departments or programs, until, finally, the effects may present themselves in courses, programs, or departments where no faculty actually participated in the faculty development event or initiative that began the faculty learning process.

Evidence for Spread of Effect beyond Single Faculty and Discussion

While persistence and growth over time leverage the impact of professional development experiences over time as an individual faculty member teaches more and more students and effects spread across their full teaching portfolio, spread of knowledge among faculty multiplies this impact even more radically. Data from both campuses provide evidence for one of the most important findings of this project: that faculty development impacts everyone within a faculty community. At Carleton, with only 234 faculty, there is one faculty community. At WSU, multiple faculty communities are located in departments and colleges that may be relatively isolated from one another.

WSU's Critical Thinking Project, a comprehensive effort directly impacting 330 of the 1,900 faculty on campus, was designed more than a decade ago to spread its impact beyond the original participants. Each participant committed to offering at least one faculty development event in the participant's home department. These events ranged from brown-bag chats about their work in the project to two- or three-day formal workshops, held with the assistance of project directors. In one case—the School of Veterinary Medicine—this extension of the project took the form of revising the clinical curriculum, in the process training all the clinical faculty to use a critical thinking approach to the diagnosis and treatment of animals. To be sure, the great majority of these events were one-shot conversations or mini-workshops about building better assignments. But two schools—Veterinary Medicine and the College of Agricultural, Human, and Natural Resource Sciences (CAHNRS)—adopted critical thinking as an outcome throughout their curricula and provided multiple opportunities for departments and individual faculty to improve their teaching around this highly valued outcome. These two units alone account for twelve of WSU's fifty-six total departments. In addition, interviews revealed that six more departments in response to the campus-wide discussion of the Critical Thinking Project added to the lists of outcomes for concentrators and graduate programs a critical thinking outcome that was specifically tailored to their disciplines. Even in three departments—Teaching and Learning, Construction Management (now the School of Design and Construction), and Kinesiology (now Kinesiology and Exercise Science)—that had not participated formally in the Project, interviews revealed that they had added such outcomes as a result of learning about the Project. Their implementations are tailored to their disciplines and existing curricula in ways that suggest the influence of the Project (though admittedly, such a distinction is hard to make at this remove). Further, during the years the Project was active, these departments offered their own faculty development opportunities, independent of any contact with the Project itself. These examples of initiatives coming out of the woodwork demonstrate that some sort of critical mass of attention to a given outcome produces a spread of effect that reaches beyond the official institutional efforts. Once the fluoride is in the water, it benefits everyone.

At the faculty level, there is evidence for this kind of spread in interviews with low-participating faculty. Twenty-eight faculty—who were selected for study because they had not enrolled for events sponsored by the Center for Teaching, Learning, and Technology, nor had they participated in the Critical Thinking Project, Writing Across the Curriculum (WAC) workshops, or portfolio review—presented syllabi, assignments, and testimony that indicate that even faculty who attend very few formal development events pick up on the initiatives that their more active colleagues have discovered. Fifteen of these participants' syllabi listed writing and/or critical thinking as outcomes for their courses.

Measuring the further spread of effect of WAC workshops is more difficult as the primary measure of impact is the implementation of new Writing in the Major [M] courses. On the one hand, faculty may choose to come to a WAC workshop because they want to increase the writing in their course. On the other hand, all departments are required to offer at least two [M] courses, providing an independent motivation for implementation. Thus, many faculty implement [M] courses without participating in the WAC workshop program. Indeed, three of the twenty low-participating faculty interviewed had taught [M] courses without ever attending a WAC workshop. While none of the three provided a syllabus or assignments from an [M] course for this research, the three indicated that they had taken over the course from a colleague and had modeled their own course materials on what the colleague had done. In two of these cases, the colleague had retired so was unavailable for consultation. In the remaining case, the new teacher frequently consulted with her colleague during her first iteration of the course, and did so less frequently in subsequent iterations. In none of the three cases did the new teachers stray far from their predecessors' methods, content, or assignments. These data are scant, but they indicate that when the curricular change leads an initiative, faculty interest may follow (the total attendance of 1,123 faculty over the span of WSU's WAC workshop offerings is powerful testimony to that effect), and that effects continue to spread via casual routes for faculty development as well, though not in as robust a manner as when the development is more intensive and when it follows faculty interest, rather than being imposed by institutional mandate.

Within Carleton's relatively small community of faculty, the spread of practices to faculty who were not part of the original development event or initiative is even more pronounced. The Higher Education Research Institute's (Hurtado et al. 2012) faculty survey results for Carleton show that the majority of faculty respondents were concerned with teaching students learning goals emphasized in WAC and QuIRK, such as critical thinking skills, how to use and evaluate data, how to seek help when needed, and how to revise papers.

According to one former Learning and Teaching Center director, even faculty who rarely attended professional development opportunities still integrated some of the faculty development programs' lessons into their teaching through their interactions with faculty and students on campus. An in-depth look at Professor Smith (not her real name), a relatively low participator in WAC and QuIRK workshops at Carleton, illuminates this statement.

While Smith, a natural scientist, was a regular attendee of LTC lunches (fourteen events from 2007 to 2011) and curriculum-related workshops and was a leader of student-support programs, she did not participate in as many forms of WAC and QuIRK programming as did other case study faculty. Nonetheless, she included many of the same WAC and QuIRK pedagogies in her freshman seminar. These pedagogies included the following:

- scaffolding assignments over the term
- helping students evaluate and use numerate data
- supporting students in creating visual representations of numerate data
- helping students write for a more general audience
- encouraging students to seek help from the Write Place, Math Center, and library, among other sources

This entirely new course was Smith's first freshman seminar and her first interdisciplinary course in twelve years at Carleton. In order to have included so many WAC/QuIRK practices, one may infer that Professor Smith designed her new course in an environment that was infused with "WAC and QuIRK" ideas that had spread beyond specific individual workshops and activities. Further evidence of WAC/QuIRK influence can be found in Smith's end-of-term evaluations. Students gave the course high ratings on the WAC and QuIRK-related topics of research, critical thinking, writing, and working with numerate data.

On the WSU campus, Smith would be a high participator, but at Carleton, her attendance at faculty development events puts her on the lower end of the continuum. Still, the common values, desirable outcomes, and signature pedagogies disseminated at those meetings are so heavily infused across the campus that even someone whose direct contact with these events and initiatives is relatively slight not only builds them into her courses, but does so well enough to earn high evaluations on those practices.

How Impacts Spread across Campus

The precise ways that the effects of faculty development efforts may spread will differ according to a given campus's culture and the visibility of the development outcomes. Interviewing faculty at these two very different institutions led to an inventory of the channels through which these outcomes diffuse throughout the campuses. For these two campuses, the list is exhaustive, though it is certainly not definitive. However, it shows the way to helping readers think about possible channels of distribution on their own campuses, where it is likely there are vectors that didn't exist in this study.

Colleague-to-colleague channels are ubiquitously described at both Carleton and WSU: faculty talk to one another about teaching. At Carleton, the combination of a small community and a college-wide, faculty-led priority on faculty development allows for richer diffusion of the topics introduced in formal development events. These topics form the core of a signature pedagogy that formal faculty development initiatives such as WAC, QuIRK, and the Writing Portfolio communicate to faculty colleagues who do and do not participate in formal events. That informal kind of spread also occurs at WSU, and researchers suspect that it is a common feature of any institution where teaching is a priority—which is to say, virtually every institution.

At Carleton, these channels are enhanced by events offered by The Perlman Center for Learning and Teaching (LTC). The LTC, originally established by the college administration (with assistance from an outside coordinator, Peter Frederick, then of Wabash College), has been faculty led since 1992. It offers weekly luncheons, book groups, and other activities that provide opportunities for faculty networking across the campus.

Faculty development initiatives such as the writing program and quantitative reasoning—that include analyzing student course work—also facilitate a larger view of student learning. Faculty accept that they are collectively responsible for students' learning rather than seeing themselves as teaching in silos. These programs promote an understanding of student learning as a process with an emphasis on providing students with multiple opportunities for learning particular skills (e.g., writing and quantitative reasoning). Faculty who participate in the portfolio sessions often leave with an idea of how they can better integrate these opportunities in widely disparate kinds of courses after learning more about how writing/epistemology in their discipline may differ from other disciplines (see Lea and Street 1988 for discussion of academic literacies). For example, one faculty member in the English department revealed that the quantitative reasoning program had inspired her to include more assignments that helped her students use quantitative data and reasoning, and to consult a friend in the psychology department in order to become more familiar with quantitative analysis herself. According to the instructor, she was able to help her students (and herself) more thoroughly interrogate quantitative data and analyses in their social science readings. In the past, she and the students would have skimmed these data or simply accepted them as fact.

Another vector for dissemination of ideas is students, who communicate effective teaching strategies from one class to another. This pathway existed primarily at Carleton, perhaps because class sizes and the overall size of the institution more readily enable such cross-fertilizations. Students experience a range of teaching styles even within a single term, let alone over their years at Carleton. Both at LTC events and in discussion with faculty, they often talk about one professor's assignments or classroom techniques while in another professor's classroom. Indeed, faculty indicate that such conversations deliver powerful incentives to try out new techniques; students rarely discuss pedagogical disasters with faculty, but they fairly often discuss techniques or assignments that they believe work well. They talk about powerful learning experiences.

Beyond informal events and conversations, other common institutional practices that are not necessarily focused on improving teaching reinforce the goals of faculty development. Faculty promotion processes, for example, include elements of faculty development. Two senior Carleton faculty members described learning from their junior colleagues while observing their classes for third-year and tenure reviews. The conversations between the observers and those observed after class provided potential for learning on both sides. In addition, both third-year and tenure reviews at Carleton include student evaluations and discussions about student learning—with department chairs and the dean of the college—based on these very detailed evaluations. As part of the evaluation process, classroom evaluation forms require Carleton students to define what they think of as ideal teaching (including a call for fully developed descriptions and names of faculty who exemplify this description) and then to compare the particular faculty member being reviewed to this ideal. Granted, this form of routine faculty development occurs in a high stakes form for the central participants, making it problematic in some ways. Still, building an emphasis on improving teaching into the evaluation process clarifies the institutional priority on teaching, and it provides an occasion for low-participating faculty to hear from colleagues and students about their strengths and needs in the classroom. Finally, both documents and conversations provide a vector for spread of effect with regard to specific pedagogical methods that are in common use at Carleton.

Another example illustrates the potentially important role that departmental reviews have had on spreading information about teaching and learning among faculty. A visit to one faculty member's office, who participated in very few workshops and who claimed not to have changed much in his teaching for more than twenty years, nonetheless illustrates the extent to which language and ideas spread across the campus. This faculty member pointed out that teaching at Carleton had changed since he arrived at the college, but stated that he was satisfied with student learning in his courses. He explained that he did not always agree with the newer ways that his colleagues taught. For instance, he was aware of faculty in his department and in the college who used rubrics for assessing student work in their courses, but he believed that these faculty were using rubrics as crutches to avoid potential student disputes over grades. He believes that grades based on a rubric are just as subjective as ratings made without a formal rubric because faculty are still making judgments in relation to each element of the rubric. Instead, he prefers to compare students' learning to one another in a particular classroom (and not to elements in a rubric) so that the students could see how much better or worse they were doing in relation to one another. Whether or not faculty in the college agree with this faculty member's pedagogical practices or his views about rubrics, clearly he is familiar with pedagogical practices outside of his own courses, and he had put some thought into determining whether these practices would be useful to him. Equally clearly, student learning matters to him (as evidenced by his choice to engage the researcher in a conversation about pedagogy rather than turn her out of his office).

Later interviews with faculty in the same department revealed that the department had just undergone a somewhat difficult evaluation process in which he and his colleagues were finally able to agree on their department's student learning outcomes and on ways of assessing these outcomes. The department's difficulties in agreeing on these learning outcomes stemmed from key differences in views about the goal of studying in this particular field. This disagreement caused the group of faculty to question their most basic assumptions about their field of study and to (re)envision departmental goals for, and assessment of, student learning. This difficult process informed the senior faculty member's consideration of rubrics and his concerns about assessing learning. Thus, even in cases where change does not occur, faculty are aware of—and contend with—the material aspects of Carleton's widespread formal faculty development programming.

At WSU, low-participating faculty offered a range of sources for elements of their course designs that reflected Critical Thinking Project priorities: conversations with colleagues whom they saw as good teachers, department meetings where faculty discussed and voted on outcomes for their majors and graduate programs, service on their department's undergraduate or graduate curriculum committees (where outcomes were discussed as well), or, in two cases, testimony that the faculty member had "heard about [the Critical Thinking Project] somewhere and thought it sounded like a good idea."

This range of responses from such a wide variety of faculty lends great confidence to the findings that gains from effective faculty development not only persist in the individual faculty members' practices, but spread throughout their practices and beyond. Ultimately, those effects can reach as high as a college's overall curriculum and methods for measuring outcomes, or they can be as humble as spreading to the colleague down the hall who hears new ideas over lunch or at coffee. Thus, intensive, multi-year efforts such as the Critical Thinking Project at WSU or the WAC and QuIRK initiatives at Carleton produce effects that extend well beyond the faculty who participate directly. Spread of effect needs to be designed into a project, and it needs to be accounted for in judging the project's ultimate worth.

The Role of Institutional Structures and Culture in Promoting or Inhibiting Spread of Effect

Formal faculty development initiatives—with agendas that extend beyond single events—arise in both top-down and grassroots fashion. At WSU, the Critical Thinking Project is a prime example of the latter, having arisen from faculty raters' perceptions that not much critical thinking was going on in students' Junior Writing Portfolios. Similarly, faculty at Carleton who were interested in improving students' quantitative reasoning established the QuIRK initiative. Grassroots initiatives like the Critical Thinking Project arise out of commonly shared faculty values. Faculty want their students to develop any number of overarching competencies and literacies: critical thinking, writing, research; visual or mathematical literacies; persistence, resourcefulness, and responsibility for one's own learning. These faculty-led initiatives tend to involve ongoing development, since they target learning outcomes that most faculty want to promote in students, and since the sheer number of faculty renders a one-shot or even one-year process impossible. While such efforts are often quite diverse in origin, some kind of teaching and learning center is most often the central hub of the action, though that office may collaborate extensively with other units.

At WSU, the Critical Thinking Project and WAC initiatives provide classic examples of such mainstream efforts. Faculty looked to CTLT and the Campus Writing Programs for leadership, with development consisting of a wide range of expert-led formal workshops, presentations and workshops led by faculty participants, and formal and informal consultations. In such cases, the unit leading the effort collaborates extensively with departments and programs in a decentralized effort that makes logistical sense (other than the basketball arena, no single facility could house a meeting of WSU's entire faculty) as well as epistemological and pedagogical sense. Engineers and philosophers think, write, and teach in different ways; hence, workshops need to meet them on their own epistemological turfs.

In the absence of a unit dedicated to faculty development around teaching and learning—currently the case at WSU—faculty development occurs at the college, departmental, or program level. Examples of all three are apparent at WSU. The College of Agriculture, Human, and Natural Resource Sciences, for example has established its own teaching and learning center. As noted earlier, the critical thinking faculty participants from the college took their learning back into their departments so strongly that it established its own set of baccalaureate outcomes—based on but not limited to WSU's Six Goals for the Baccalaureate—and their efforts are entirely faculty led. The Department of Teaching and Learning in the School of Education was one of the units where the critical thinking work spread without formal connections to the project. There, department faculty established a set of learning outcomes for their concentrators and planned as a faculty a set of workshops and other events that helped them promote those outcomes in their students' work. Finally, on the program level, the English department's composition program has set up regular Professional Development Opportunities—roughly twenty hour-long events per academic year—that address the common goals and outcomes for teaching composition, from first-year writing to senior-level courses in professional and technical writing. These venues do not attempt to reach across the campus, as a teaching and learning center would do, but they provide faculty in their units with development events and consultations centered on learning outcomes that are appropriate to the common values and interests of college, departmental, or program faculty.

Carleton exemplifies the power of a robust, fully integrated set of reinforcing activities that promote effective teaching. Formal professional development events provide multiple, intertwining pathways for faculty to learn about pedagogies that are highly valued by both the faculty and the institution. Respect for these pedagogies is built into administrative processes such as annual review, tenure and promotion, and departmental or program review processes. At Carleton even top-down values and strategies meet with grassroots, faculty-led events or initiatives in a seamless connection that creates a highly functioning academic community.

At Carleton, faculty development begins immediately, with Orientation and Winter Workshops for new faculty. In five interviews, faculty made specific comments about how Carleton, in general, expected new faculty members to be innovative in their teaching and to participate in faculty development activities. For example, two mid- to late-career faculty members described faculty development attendance as a responsibility and obligation for newer hires. One said,

> I think there's a sort of a general climate at Carleton, especially when you're unten-ured, there's a sort of finding out what pedagogical best practice is—[it] is quite important and is one of your responsibilities. And so when that's available, in an area that you're concerned with, I think there's a sort of a natural tendency to think you ought to take it up.

The other faculty member said that he, in particular, would tell junior colleagues to attend faculty development events because

> maybe you don't need to do all these things, and some of them are really not going to be very helpful for you or effective uses of your time, let's put it that way. But you do need to do some of these things, again, in part because they will have real benefits for your teaching, but also because, again, you get these sort of political benefits, if you will, of your sort of acting like a good citizen.

This emphasis on faculty development as good citizenship developed over a period of discontent over the curriculum that resulted in establishing a learning and teaching center (the Perlman Center for Learning and Teaching), reforming the writing require-ments, and installing a mid-career writing portfolio. A series of three Bush Founda-tion grants provided funding for a range of faculty development—indeed, though the grant funded startup costs for the writing portfolio, its central purpose was faculty development around writing. Success there led to other initiatives, including secur-ing FIPSE funding for QuIRK. Each faculty-led initiative came with its own faculty development as a way of diffusing the initiative throughout the community. Over the ten-year period between 1997 and 2007, faculty development became a centerpiece of Carleton life, engaged in by faculty, staff, and students alike.

By the time of this study, New Faculty Orientation had been transformed so that it initiated these community priorities. Today, new faculty members learn about employee-oriented information (e.g., sexual harassment policies) and expectations and support for their teaching. At the 2009 orientation, Carleton's highest officers emphasized faculty members' role in teaching, among their other duties of pursuing scholarship and college service. One of the first comments that Carleton's president made to the group was that he thought that the research and teaching balance at the school was "just right." He said that faculty members who were "good" teachers could not help doing their research and contributing to what counted as knowledge in their disciplines. Returning to issues of teaching, the dean explained changes in Carleton's student curriculum, including new quantitative reasoning requirements and writing-rich courses—both of which were influenced by the WAC and QuIRK faculty develop-ment programs. Further speakers included the director of the Writing Program (and WAC), reference librarians, academic technologists, a panel of faculty from a range of ages and experience levels, and a panel of students with advice on teaching and work-ing with students. From top to bottom, then, teaching had become the central focus of the orientation, and the message was clear: good teaching matters, and the college provides many venues for improving one's teaching.

The New Faculty Winter Workshop, after the first academic term of the year, featured even more intensive faculty development related to teaching. These workshops were hosted by the LTC director, with some collaboration from other faculty and an associate dean of the college. The LTC director in 2009 explained that his overarching goal for the workshop was to instill in new faculty an understanding that it was their professional duty to develop their teaching skills. The workshop bore out his goal with hands-on teaching activities and constructive critiques, discussions about assignment design (including the WAC director's presentation on developing writing assignments), discussions about grants (including WAC and QuIRK curriculum development grants), and assessment of student learning. In end-of-workshop surveys of sixteen participants, twelve were most appreciative of the micro-teaching activities and three hoped to (re)design their writing assignments, in particular. Faculty members in the new faculty winter workshop and orientation—whether temporary, adjunct, or tenure-track—often formed friendships and support networks that lasted even beyond their time at Carleton. A faculty member who had worked at Carleton for more than eight years said that he still had a bond with his colleagues in the group. This statement was confirmed by both newer and more senior faculty at the college. Friends from the 2009 cohort are still engaging with one another online—as well as in person—even though at least one is now at a different institution out of state.

This shared beginning introduces participants to a robust set of development activities. Several faculty at Carleton described the effects of these activities. A newer faculty member's story illustrates Carleton's enculturation of new faculty through its active intellectual community around teaching and learning issues (particularly in relation to practices promoted by faculty development programs), at the same time that the story shows how difficult it is to trace changes in teaching directly back to individual workshops, events, program leaders, or colleagues.

In an informal 2011 social encounter, William (pseudonym), completely unsolicited, asked a Tracer researcher if she would like to hear about the courses he was putting together for the upcoming term. As he opened his binder and turned to the freshman seminar he was designing, William explained that he was still moving assignments and readings around in order to best develop the students' knowledge base and writing throughout the term. He decided to begin by asking students to write smaller, focused assignments that would lead up to a larger research paper. William then built in time for students to talk to him about their papers, to bring in drafts of their research papers for in-class peer reviews, and to meet with a librarian about their research. He also included a grading rubric with the syllabus. In an upper division course that he was also teaching that term, he included on his course website (Moodle) an anonymous paper from a past course with his comments and grade still on it, course and assignment learning goals, and links to his department's learning goals and writing guidelines. When the researcher asked William whether he had used such practices in his past teaching—as a graduate student or in a year-long position at a state university—he answered that Carleton had shaped most of his teaching practices (other than requiring drafts). He did not remember who at Carleton had told him about grading rubrics, scaffolding, or learning goals, but he regularly sought advice from others in his department. Nonetheless, he believed but was not entirely sure that he had learned "a great deal" from the new faculty winter workshop during his first year at Carleton. William is by no means aberrant in his teaching practices and assiduous attention to teaching at Carleton. His concern with scaffolding students' learning in the course, writing, informational literacy, clear expectations for student work, and peer collaboration in the classroom are practices that Carleton's faculty development programs have long promoted.

It is important to note that William had only been at Carleton a little more than one academic year, yet he had attended approximately two of the weekly LTC lunches, two of the larger-scale formal faculty development programs during the college's winter break, the New Faculty Winter Workshop, and the 2011 Writing Program student portfolio rating session. Although faculty in his department are not known for participating in faculty development activities—as two others from his department confirmed—William reported that he knew he would have to become a better teacher after attending the New Faculty Orientation before his first year of teaching at Carleton. He described the orientation's message as consisting primarily of advice about teaching rather than about research. Nonetheless, this does not mean that William ignored his own scholarly interests; he was just as excited to discuss his research and course material as he was to talk about his teaching practices.

William exemplifies the faculty interviewed at Carleton. Whether they come from departments that actively participate in faculty development or ones that rarely do, the message that teaching matters, the priorities faculty have established around certain learning outcomes—writing, quantitative reasoning, and so forth—and the need to develop teaching strategies that fit his courses, his students, his discipline, and the expectations of the institution have clearly sunk in for William. He and his colleagues actively pursue better teaching methods, and those methods show up in their descriptions of practices, as well as in their course syllabi and materials. Finally, William's experience testifies to the ready availability of faculty development opportunities and resources, and to the fact that newer and more senior faculty, staff, and even students take advantage of what Carleton offers.

Even the hiring process at Carleton establishes these teaching priorities. Although many new faculty such as William need to learn and develop their teaching skills once they arrive at Carleton, they are usually (except in very rare but significant cases) aware of Carleton's emphasis on teaching at a small, liberal arts college with very competitive admissions policies. When hiring, faculty chairs and deans also emphasize the importance of both teaching and scholarship in faculty employment at the college. In job interviews, prospective faculty members receive multiple messages about the importance of developing their teaching as well as scholarship. The full-page handout given to tenure-track interviewees even overtly supports faculty development as part of their teaching and research development. The handout specifically mentions the possibility of obtaining grants from faculty development initiatives such as WAC, QuIRK, and Viz (a new Visuality initiative funded by the Mellon Foundation), and describes LTC programming and the December micro-teaching activity for new faculty. In addition, tenure-track faculty receive a copy of "What You Should Know: An Open Letter to New PhDs" from the Academic Deans of the Commonwealth Partnership (Smith et al. 1996). The very first note to new PhDs is that "the teachers we want to attract are first and foremost committed to the advancement of learning." Even the small number of temporary faculty are recruited with similar priorities. In the fall term of 2009, interviewees for appointments of less than one year and for one to two years were all given a short handout describing Carleton's support for their "professional activities." These activities included the New Faculty Orientation and LTC programming. Both handouts stated that "we are interested in your professional development and renewal and want to support your needs and interests."

One interviewee, who had been involved in hiring faculty at Carleton over the past five years, reiterated these messages about the importance of developing teaching skills, as well as research. The interviewee said that candidates who applied to Carleton were usually attracted because of the college's teaching focus, and were amazed by the array of professional development opportunities. Discussions with four current and former department chairs about their hiring practices unearthed a mixture of concerns about teaching skills (or potential skills) and research interests. None of the four interviewees could be described as high participators. All four chairs stressed the importance of hiring faculty members who are (or show the potential of becoming) good teachers, and they stressed to different degrees the extent to which they prioritized teaching quality together with concerns over candidates' disciplinary scholarship. Two of the chairs articulated the importance of hiring someone who has liberal arts experience, who knowledgeably describes a teaching philosophy, and who shows a passion for teaching as well as research. One faculty member said that he had had trouble with new hires or potential hires who really didn't know how much time they would be expected to spend with undergraduates at Carleton (as opposed to other places). He also emphasized the importance of hiring individuals in his field who were energetic teachers and who did not have what he characterized as the egotistical attitude that (he says) is stereotypical of his field. Given the emphasis on teaching and the information about faculty development presented during the hiring process, new faculty arrive already primed to take advantage of the many resources the college makes available to them.

Carleton's high level of faculty development participation does not occur without controversy—faculty, after all, are rarely unanimous about anything—but even the detractors exhibit the effects of Carleton's rich menu of options. Two interviewees—a current chair and a former chair of one social science department—were critical of what they saw as Carleton's excessive concern with faculty development for teaching and relatively little attention to faculty research interests. Still, these responses did not reflect a lack of concern about teaching. One interviewee agreed that quality teaching was important, and she supported the many forms of informal faculty development that existed at the college (third-year review and tenure observations [which benefit older as well as younger faculty], discussions among colleagues, and faculty mentoring). She said that so many formal faculty development opportunities made them seem ordinary or insignificant, so that she was tempted to ignore them. Ultimately, she was concerned that she was unable to live up to all the expectations she felt were placed on her—as a woman with a family and as a faculty member at Carleton.

The second interviewee spoke strongly against Carleton's proliferation of faculty development activities related to teaching and what he saw as a lack of attention to faculty members' research needs. He wanted to institute a departmental gathering for faculty to share their research with one another. Nevertheless, while he said that he thought he was a better teacher when he was busy writing a book as well as teaching, he attended more faculty development activities after the interview, and he provided the Tracer Project with some useful artifacts of assignment prompts for our study. These detractors reflect how extensive the offerings are—so many that they can seem overwhelming or unbalancing with relation to faculty research—yet even these detractors discuss (and demonstrate via course documents) ways their teaching has improved as a result of their awareness of the priorities and practices rehearsed in formal faculty development.

In addition to infusing its community with formal faculty development resources and opportunities, many of these activities occur in collaboration with staff and students. Thus, librarians are fully aware of the kinds of assignments faculty are making, so they can assist faculty in making the assignments better, and stand ready to help students meet high faculty expectations. Similarly, when faculty want to make technology-heavy assignments, information technology staff are there to recommend the best technologies for a given assignment, to help faculty learn what they need to know in order to make the assignment work, and to help students acquire whatever technical knowledge they might need in order to fulfill the assignment.

Portfolio Rating and Spread of Effect

Whether portfolio rating is conceived as faculty development, as at Carleton, or not, as at WSU, this process provides a rich setting for faculty conversations about common expectations, best practices in assigning writing, setting high standards for students, and so forth. Probably any local evaluation of students' performances along a given learning dimension would do the same. Such is the value of keeping a learning assessment process local: the teaching faculty see a wide range of student performances, and the collaborative environment for rating student learning outcomes provides ample opportunities for teacher discussion around those outcomes.

At WSU, raters from across the university engage in a series of rating sessions, each one engaging a varying set of raters. The process involves raters deciding whether to assign a rating of "Needs Work," "Pass," or "Pass with Distinction" to the portfolio in front of them. Two moments in this process encourage raters to talk with each other. The first is the norming session that begins each rating session. Norming involves reading and discussing one or two previously scored portfolios. Conversations involve faculty raters in discussions of the qualities of the student's writing, in areas of strength and need, and in locating that performance on the scale from "Needs Work" to "Pass with Distinction." Frequently, discussions also engage raters in talking about disciplinary differences ("Is this really excellent writing for an engineering student?"), speculations about the assignment ("Was this student actually challenged to do her best work?"), grading practices ("This rubric seems to value content rather than effective writing"), and, perhaps most telling, a great deal about how raters might encourage their own students to write as effectively as the student whose portfolio is in front of them. The second location for teacher talk occurs when raters have disagreed on a result and are required to consult with each other in order to resolve the split. Quite often, such disagreements arise when one rater encounters student writing from a very different discipline from the rater's own (Condon and Leonhardy 2001), or when the quality of the student's writing varies substantially from one paper to another. In weighing the student's overall performance, raters almost always bring their own experiences in assigning and evaluating writing to bear on the mutual decision they have to make. All these conversations provide opportunities for raters to discuss their own practices, to think together about appropriate standards for students' performances at various levels (writing may come from first- or second-year courses, or from upper-division ones) in the curriculum or in different disciplines. Interviews with WSU portfolio raters indicated that they valued these discussions to the point that thirty-three of the forty raters in the study mentioned this teacher talk as a primary reason for continuing as raters. What they learned in rating sessions affected their own teaching practices, and rating sessions caused faculty to share their own inferences and successes among the group. Since approximately 500 WSU faculty have participated as raters at one time or another, rating sessions provide a powerful spread of effect at a large university.

At Carleton, the rating process was modeled on WSU's, though the portfolio design differs. Each year's group of 35–40 raters gather for a norming session at the beginning of the three-day rating process, and raters who disagree on a portfolio engage in a consultation to make the final determination, which, as at WSU, is "Needs

Work," "Pass," or "Exemplary." However, Carleton's portfolio process was designed to incorporate faculty development. Carleton students have to attend to a formula for portfolio contents: for example, portfolios must contain writing from three different departments or programs at the college, and they must contain at least one thesis-driven paper and one that is grounded in observation. Finally, and crucially, Carleton students must include a copy of the original assignment with each written product in the portfolio.

These differences provide even greater impetus for spread of effect. For three half-days each June, 12–15 percent of Carleton's faculty sit together to read and in many cases discuss students' written performances to specific assignments. All these raters can see how their colleagues' assignments have (or have not) produced student responses that are a pleasure to read, and they can see how their colleagues have incorporated the learning goals that the college's faculty development initiatives promote. One early signal that spread of effect was a powerful outcome of the rating process occurred during the first year of rating, when many students included in their portfolios a field observation lab report about chokecherries, using data collected in the college's arboretum. The assignment was of the "recipe" variety, and the papers displayed a marked lack of originality. After reading the fourth or fifth portfolio containing a chokecherry paper, faculty began to grumble, then sigh, and finally to express their anguish in various audible ways. The resulting discussion engaged raters from across the college with faculty from the department that offered this lab course. Over the next few years, the assignment was revised into one that provided students with more guidance and asked them to pose and solve a problem grounded in their observations in the arboretum. The powerful nature of Carleton's rating process as an agent for spreading the effects of faculty development illustrates how an institution can multiply the effects of a routine event—rating portfolios—by designing that event around faculty development objectives.

The Role of Generative Cultures of Teaching and Learning

Every institution has a culture of teaching and learning. The difference among institutions, or even parts of larger institutions, lies in how generative that culture proves to be. The data above demonstrate some of the differences between small institutions, where one can speak of *a* culture of teaching and learning, and large ones, where one thinks in terms of *cultures* of teaching and learning. The differences can be stark, but as the data show, there are common elements to consider. On both campuses, for example, faculty care deeply about teaching and work to improve their teaching. Even the most reluctant faculty members realize that teaching matters in their annual reviews, in tenure and promotion, and in merit raises, so even the few who are unwilling to attend formal development events see that being good teachers is in their enlightened self-interest. That self-interest explains the presence of a culture of teaching and learning. But what actions or attitudes can make that culture more generative?

If faculty members are open to change and are willing to experiment with their teaching, then change can happen more quickly, and it can spread more widely among faculty colleagues. Factors that encourage a willingness to experiment range widely. Every campus is likely to have a group of "usual suspects"—faculty who thrive on teaching and who constantly seek out ways to improve, or simply try out new methods to keep life interesting. To the extent that these faculty can become exemplars, an institution encourages more faculty to take risks in the classroom and to share the results, good or bad, with their colleagues. The faculty at a small liberal arts college know who these experimenters are. They are visible in ways that they are not at large institutions. They lead new initiatives. They lead brown bag discussions. They introduce the outside experts. They support change. And because they are so visible, what they do is well known and can be widely imitated. At a larger institution, such teachers are still well known within their home departments, to much the same effect as in small colleges, and the institution can promote their visibility in many ways. WSU's establishment of a President's Teaching Academy began with identifying twenty-five teachers—two from each college, with additions from the branch campuses—who were recognized as the best teachers. These exemplars took on the role of promoting a generative culture of teaching and learning across the campus. One of their earliest achievements was designing the Six Goals for the Baccalaureate and successfully pushing for Faculty Senate approval. And on both campuses, establishing financial support and/or campus recognition for innovation in teaching encourages a wider range of faculty to join the ranks of the experimenters.

As faculty become more open to change, a menu of faculty development opportunities helps keep them engaged. The Carleton data demonstrate a kind of snowballing effect for formal faculty development. LTC events, external grants centered on faculty development around curricular changes, and a regular program of outside experts quickly create a buzz about teaching that in turn promotes attendance at formal development events. Very early in the process of revising the writing curriculum at Carleton, Condon gave a campus-wide workshop that drew nine faculty—all usual suspects. Three years later, he and Rutz gave a workshop on working with students who are non-native speakers of English—a much narrower focus than that first workshop—which drew thirty-one participants, or one-sixth of Carleton's total faculty at the time. Today, LTC luncheon events regularly draw forty to fifty faculty, staff, and students, and there are twenty-five to thirty formal opportunities per year that are open to all faculty. More opportunities exist within individual departments.

Similarly, the Critical Thinking Project at WSU was designed to target a learning outcome that faculty strongly supported, and so it rapidly moved beyond the usual suspects, ultimately working with 330 faculty—roughly one-fourth of WSU's total at the time. The requirement that each participant offer an event within his or her own unit spread the effect. The result is that even a decade later, faculty are still not only using what they learned during that project, they continue to experiment. The Project taught them better ways of teaching critical thinking, but it also taught them how to innovate, make changes, measure effects, and engage in a process of continuous improvement. The first step in such a success lies in having a menu of opportunities for improvement available.

An allied factor is building a support structure for improving teaching that goes beyond formal faculty development. Events serve several important purposes. They provide an opportunity to publicize a priority, for example, as well as a chance for faculty to work with each other on those priorities or to work with outside experts. But single events, even at small places like Carleton, reach a relatively small number of faculty. To be fully effective, such events need to exist within a context of support for those priorities that helps infuse them throughout the institution. The events become the public face of a range of resources. Large institutions tend to spend money on initiatives that promise to affect large numbers of students, so these grants focused on department- or program-level change. At Carleton, such funding reaches individual faculty, with mini-grants to support developing new courses or revising existing courses to address broad outcomes like writing, quantitative reasoning, and visual literacy. Formal events draw the community's attention to common goals, and they may act as a kind of gateway to further resources such as mini-grants, expert consultations, working groups of colleagues, and so forth. Institutions, especially large ones, express their actual values by means of their budgets (LeLoup and Shull 2002). This wide range of support establishes that the institution promotes experimentation not just by lip service but with resources.

Another result of providing robust support is the message that working on one's teaching is actually an acceptable thing to do. If all the support and all the talk is about research, then faculty hear that message. But if half the messaging is about teaching, faculty hear that, too. One quick experiment can help pinpoint where the conversation is on a given campus. If one were to sit down with a colleague at WSU, the conversation is almost certain to turn to research. If one sits down with a colleague at Carleton, the conversation is at least as likely to focus on teaching. That difference is an outcome of the messages administrators and colleagues send. At a large, PhD-extensive state land grant university, central administration strongly promotes research—particularly the kind that attracts grant funding that can ease budget constraints. Therefore, while WSU holds to the 40–40–20 proportion of teaching-research-service that is common among such universities, WSU faculty clearly indicated that research counted the most for them, and that teaching, while not irrelevant, was clearly subordinate in the reward structures. Messages matter—and the wrong message can even controvert the institution's plainly stated weighting of criteria for annual review, tenure, and promotion.

In addition to conscious messaging, the evaluative structures that are in place need to acknowledge the difficulties inherent in changing one's pedagogy. In any case, innovation is a longer process than many people think. Almost uniformly, the first iteration is never an unqualified success, and course evaluations may reflect that fact. WSU's Critical Thinking Project shepherded faculty through two iterations of their new practices and provided support from colleagues and experts in helping faculty develop ways of knowing what was working and what needed to change. As interviews revealed, this last lesson may have been the most important, since most faculty not only continued to innovate, but indicated that what they learned about self-evaluation, classroom assessment techniques, and student feedback allowed them to continue the change process with confidence. Still, such structures as annual review need to account for the difficulties faculty may encounter as they make changes in their courses. Valuing innovation as part of such review or allowing a faculty member to exempt a course that is under revision from the review process speaks volumes about the openness of the institution to experimentation with teaching.

Once the hiring, annual review, tenure, promotion, and other reward structures change to accommodate a faculty member's focus on teaching and to support the change process, faculty get the message that good teaching matters. One way to gauge the success of those accommodations is to examine the pervasiveness of faculty conversations about teaching and especially about outcomes or pedagogies the institution has established as desirable. In the end, faculty do not need to attend formal development events in order to get the messages about writing, quantitative reasoning, student-centered pedagogies, and the like. As one faculty member pointed out, "That stuff is in the air."

Developing an Action Agenda: A Beginning

One of the unexpected outcomes of this project was developing an understanding about what a generative, productive culture of teaching and learning among the faculty can look like. Some of the items on that list can be derived from the data collected about faculty practices; indeed, some of those items are listed above:

- Faculty display a willingness to experiment with teaching, an openness to change.
- The institution provides a menu of opportunities for changes in teaching practices.
- The support structure for improving teaching goes beyond formal faculty development to embrace routine actions and venues and to support individual faculty in their attempts to change.
- Working on teaching is clearly an acceptable thing to do on a campus.

- The institution can use a variety of measures to promote a conversation about teaching.
- Faculty exchange of ideas is an important part of the context, so that individuals making changes realize that they are not alone and so that successful changes spread among colleagues.
- "Stuff is in the air."

In addition, as the culture of teaching and learning becomes more and more productive, it promotes the spread of effect among faculty within and across departments and colleges, as well as among different institutions. Even at Carleton, where faculty turnover is relatively low, some faculty teach in more than one department or program or move to other institutions. At WSU, where faculty turnover is relatively high, and where contingent faculty often teach in several departments or programs, some consideration is due to overall factors in developing faculty as teachers.

Careers can be long and faculty move around. Some of the non-tenure-track faculty at WSU are more senior than most of their tenure-track colleagues. Two such faculty, Dr. Maialena (twenty years) and Dr. Cypress (twenty-four years), had taught at WSU longer than all but two of the tenure-track faculty research participants. Unlike those tenure-track colleagues, however, they had taught in history, world civilizations, French, art history, technical writing, creative writing, English literature, and first-year composition—in addition to working at WSU's National Public Radio station (Maialena) and mentoring the English department's creative writing students as they worked to publish their writing (Cypress). Attending to the development of contingent faculty as teachers pays even bigger dividends than helping the "permanent" faculty. Contingent faculty teach more classes per full-time employee, and their courses tend to be larger introductory sections, so each course contains more students. Yet, as reported earlier, many times contingent faculty are fearful that changes in their teaching practices will result in lower evaluations, thus potentially putting continued employment at risk. Developing support for change has perhaps its greatest impact in this group, a group that in turn arguably has the greatest impact on students.

Institutions that grant graduate degrees must consider that they are training future faculty, and our research has revealed that even smaller, undergraduate-only institutions can acknowledge that some faculty move on to teach in other schools. So all institutions to a greater or lesser degree are preparing future faculty. Just as ideas come *into* a campus, they also leave for other campuses. A robust system of faculty development and the experience of working in a productive culture of teaching and learning produces its greatest benefits on the home campus, but the reach of such a system or culture can extend far beyond the home campus.

As exploration continues of changes in student learning outcomes that are driven by changes in faculty learning, this action agenda will lengthen. For now, the primary point to emphasize is that every campus has a culture of teaching and learning that controls the ability of faculty development to improve teaching. The key concern on any campus, then, is to work with that culture to make it more productive, more effective in promoting best practices in the classroom. Effective promotion looks at the sites for faculty development: formal events, self-directed change processes, and infusion of teaching goals into routine events. Looking carefully at common goals among the faculty, building a set of varied opportunities for development that are buttressed by a network of resources to support better teaching, and broadly sharing the outcomes of those efforts can go a long way toward increasing that culture's impact.

6 Reaching Students

This PROJECT SPRANG from a deceptively simple question: When faculty change their teaching, what is the impact on student learning? After three years of mixed methods investigation, the answer is that the connection is elusive but detectable. Literature connecting faculty development to student learning, while well developed in K–12 circles, is less common in the post-secondary context. STEM disciplines document the role of interactive, small-group pedagogies as well as undergraduate research in increasing student retention (Russell, Hancock, and McCullough 2007; Nagda et al. 1998) and learning (Freeman et al. 2014; Ebert-May, Batlzi, and Weber 2006; Hoellwarth, Moelter, and Knight 2005; Laursen et al. 2010; Middlecamp 2008). Faculty professional development programs demonstrate changes of attitude and practice for program participants (Connolly and Millar 2006; Fullan 2001; Garet et al. 2001; Macdonald et al. 2004). However, as evidenced by a recent study from the National Research Council (Singer, Nielsen, and Schweingruber 2012), the need remains to link changes in practice and attitude attributed to professional development programs to gains in student learning. Using data from two campuses with long traditions of supporting faculty involvement in Writing Across the Curriculum (WAC) as well as other cross-curricular initiatives, the current study has made some connections and generated methodologies for making more. This chapter delivers the payoff from the Direct Path: faculty learn new teaching concepts and techniques; they apply that new knowledge to improve their teaching; and student learning improves as well. In verifying that the Direct Path works, locally developed instruments aligned with faculty development goals proved to be more suitable to the assessment of learning gains on a specific campus than imported instruments used without local adaptation.

Indeed, the complications involved in finding connections between what faculty learn about teaching and what students learn in those faculty members' courses reach far beyond the difficulties of finding means of detecting changes in students' work products. Most difficult of all is tracing the effects on student learning at the course level. Development or refinement of new competencies depends not just on teaching, but on time, opportunity, and a host of other confounding factors (Haswell 1991). Furthermore, faculty and students experience institutions on different temporal scales. Faculty who are learning new teaching practices may implement those practices over several iterations of a course, but students in a given iteration experience that practice in one specific term; therefore, while in some cases student learning effects are traceable via traditional research methods to individual faculty learning, in most instances institutions can more effectively seek changes in learning at the campus level, particularly over time. The Tracer Project developed its own methods to surface such changes, recognizing that methodologies must fit local contexts and that longitudinal studies and examinations of effects on a scale beyond the individual course (and therefore measuring the effects of campus-wide priorities) have a greater chance of revealing the teaching and learning mechanisms that matter over the long run. This necessarily complex three-year study points to the obligation for research designed to encompass faculty careers as well as comparative student performances.

Uncovering evidence of faculty learning that fosters and improves student learning is necessarily a longitudinal process. Nevertheless, the research methods used on both campuses provide some clues to the effects of faculty development on the classroom. The key variables are (1) the type of faculty development to be studied, (2) the methods used, and (3) the assessment instrument applied to relevant data.

The faculty development initiatives examined deal with issues that go beyond mere learning of course content. In-course assignments and tests can help determine whether students have acquired a particular set of facts or are able to apply a finite set of rules. The Tracer Project focused instead on a set of overarching competencies that students apply almost everywhere in their learning experiences: writing, higher-order thinking, and quantitative reasoning—not because these are the most important competencies, but because our two campuses had established them as priorities and have mounted significant, ongoing efforts to improve the teaching of these outcomes across their curricula. What follows includes examples in which single treatments have positively influenced students' competencies on one or more of these outcomes. But it more often presents evidence that despite detecting these changes, the timing of a single-course assessment misses a significant portion of the course's impact on a student's acquisition of the competency. Most faculty have experienced feedback from students about how something they learned from a given course has allowed them to do better in later courses—astonishingly, such feedback often comes from students who did not demonstrate that learning in the original course. Faculty interview subjects at WSU offered multiple examples of students who reported or demonstrated earlier learning in later courses. Writing teachers, in particular, know that what they teach often takes hold some time after a student has completed the writing course. Perhaps most important is the fact that such studies should target what happens in student learning, rather than on a specific course. As a whole, educators all care most that students acquire and advance a given set of competencies between matriculation and graduation. Advancing such competencies requires multiple opportunities for using them; hence, evaluating such learning should reach beyond the single course.

Multiple opportunities to acquire such competencies, then, require measurements that extend beyond course boundaries. Longitudinal studies typically follow individual students by collecting their work over a span of time (Sternglass 1997; Sommers 2006). Program reviews typically look at student performances en masse, by examining collections of students' work from different sections rather than focusing on individual students. Course portfolios work particularly well for such investigations. Finally, vertical and horizontal collections of student work products from across the curriculum offer opportunities to examine what competencies students acquire, how those competencies progress, and when (or whether) students achieve mastery. Sternglass (1997), Sommers (2006), and Haswell (2000) all provide examples of research that examines what students learn and how that learning develops over their time in college. Nancy Sommers's longitudinal study of writing at Harvard, in particular, establishes that students display their learning in a wide variety of locations, both within the curriculum—in courses or writing portfolios, for example—as well as in extracurricular locations such as fund raising for a cause, participating in multicampus initiatives such as Model UN, or following up on off-campus service learning opportunities.

Following these examples, Tracer focused on individual faculty members' practices across the courses they teach, on collections of student work products from across the curriculum, and on the search for learning outcomes that have been promoted broadly on our two campuses.

Critical Thinking at Washington State University

These complexities make following the effects of what faculty learn about teaching into student work products difficult but not impossible. Tracer Project results demonstrate that overcoming the difficulties is worth the effort—and the cost. Examining faculty learning across courses revealed some of the deeper and longer-lasting effects on faculty learning that can be accomplished through systemic faculty development. Similarly, successful faculty development can have marked effects on student learning. In general terms, our study of the sites of faculty learning at both campuses informed what researchers already know about best practice in faculty development that is geared to encourage faculty learning. The unifying theme for both campuses focuses on changing *faculty* practices by engaging faculty in a learning process about best teaching practices. The Tracer Project sought to add to that description. A successful case also begins with the intention to produce changes in student learning outcomes, with a research design that can measure such effects as they occur, and with the resources needed to accomplish those goals.

WSU's original Critical Thinking Project (1999–2003) illustrates the importance of the long-understood aspects of success as well as the additions relating to student learning outcomes. In the process of refining a rubric that the collaborators intended as a tool for institutional assessment, the team discovered a high level of interest among faculty in using the rubric as a teaching tool. In effect, the developers had tapped into a strong priority among faculty, who wanted better ways to promote higher-order thinking among their students. But when some of these faculty tried using the rubric in grading their students' work, they encountered difficulties because an instrument designed as an absolute scale that could account for gains in students' performances across time was not sufficiently specific to work in individual courses. Further development was needed to turn an assessment tool into an instructional tool.

A 1999–2000 grant from Washington's Higher Education Coordinating Board allowed the Center for Teaching, Learning, and Technology (CTLT), the Writing Programs, and the Office of General Education to pilot the new rubric (at that point entitled the WSU Guide to Rating Critical Thinking; see appendix 1) with a group of five faculty, and the results allowed WSU to secure a three-year grant from the Fund for the Improvement of Post-Secondary Education (FIPSE). During these four years, the team of collaborators worked with more than 400 faculty from all categories—tenure-track, full-time temporary, adjunct, and graduate assistants—to redesign courses to improve students' critical thinking competencies. The faculty learning process began with workshops centered on how faculty could adapt the rubric to fit their disciplines (for example, engineers added problem solving as an explicit dimension, even though problem solving correlates to dimension one at a 95 percent rate), to fit the level of their course (what faculty ask of students differs greatly between first-year, upper-division, and graduate-level courses), and to fit the culture(s) of the students they taught. Faculty members' commitment to the project lasted through two iterations of the course on which they focused. Participants also provided sets of assignments and student work products (almost uniformly, papers students had written as part of the course requirements, but also including problem sets from math or engineering, as well as case studies, posters, and other outcomes) from courses that ranged from accounting to orchard management to philosophy to zoology. These sets included a "before"— from the target course in the iteration just before the teacher's participation in the Critical Thinking Project—as well as an "after"—assignments and performances from the first and second iterations of the revised course. In cases of multiple-section courses such as World Civilizations or first-year composition, horizontal collections allowed comparisons of student work from courses in which the rubric and critical thinking methodology were being used with courses in which they were not. Participants also trained as raters, allowing the Critical Thinking Project to use the WSU Guide to Rating Critical Thinking to compare ratings from before and after the intervention, in order to measure gains produced by what the faculty had learned about teaching critical thinking. These ratings also allowed the project to determine whether faculty adap-

Comparison CT Scores Spring 2000

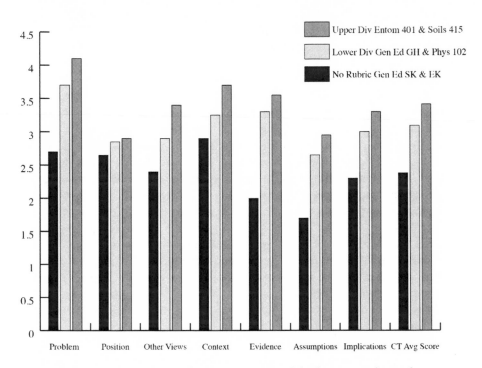

Figure 6.1. Comparisons among multiple courses. Critical thinking scores from a first-year general education course without the rubric (black bars), another section of the same course with rubric (white bars), and an upper-division course with the rubric (shaded bars).

tations of the Guide—featuring marked, even radical revisions—dampened the effects of the new pedagogies. Faculty participants also committed to offering a formal faculty development event within their home departments.

The results from four years of data, collected from faculty and courses of all kinds, at all levels, and across WSU's curriculum, were positive, to say the least. Two figures illustrate the kinds of comparison the Critical Thinking Project data allowed—before and after comparisons for different iterations of a course taught by a single faculty member and side-by-side comparisons for multiple-section courses, some of which used the Guide and some of which did not.

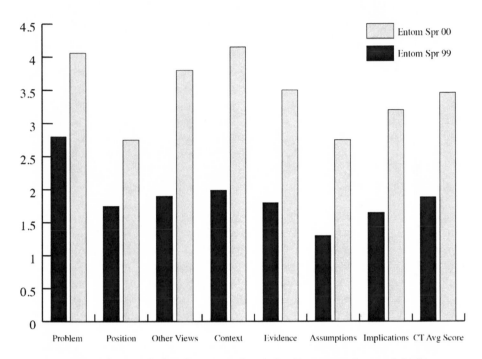

Figure 6.2. Entomology 401 before (Spring 1999) and after (Spring 2000) critical thinking adaptation. Students performed better in the "after" iteration by an average of 1.5 points on a six-point scale.

Figure 6.1 demonstrates the types of comparisons that can be made. The first comparison is between sections of World Civilizations, a multiple-section General Education course that was required of all first-year students. The figure compares student writing in the sections that did not use the Guide with sections that explicitly used the Guide. Students show higher scores on every dimension of the sections using the Guide; average scores were 2.4 in the non-rubric section and 3.1 in the section where the instructor used an adaptation of the Guide. That difference, using Pearson's Correlation Coefficient, is statistically significant (p value $< .05$). The additional comparison shown in the figure is to Entomology 401, a senior-level Writing in the

Major course where the instructor used her own adaptation of the Guide. Again, students scored higher in every dimension, for an average of 3.4—a full point higher than students in the lower division courses where the critical thinking pedagogy was employed.

Another comparison for Entomology 401 is shown in figure 6.2, which demonstrates a before-and-after result. The ratings compare student term papers from the semester *before* the instructor adapted the assignment so that it specifically addressed critical thinking and implemented a grading scale that also explicitly featured critical thinking, among other outcomes such as good writing and scientific understanding.

Independent ratings of student's learning outcomes demonstrate that when faculty learn and apply better ways of addressing desirable student learning outcomes, they translate their learning into course materials and assignments that actually do positively influence students' learning. That result, in the end, constitutes a successful case, and that kind of design produces long-range outcomes, as this chapter demonstrates.

Extending the Success: Follow-up on Critical Thinking at WSU

Another way that the original Critical Thinking Project was successful is that it established a strong baseline for later study. That baseline was one of the reasons the Tracer Project team was optimistic about finding ways to identify student learning gains in courses taught by faculty who were high participators—and why researchers were curious about whether there would be a differential between high and low participators' students. Pursuing those answers involved looking first for the easy cases: initiatives on both campuses that have addressed complex learning goals—writing, critical thinking, quantitative reasoning—that had been in place for a number of years, and that had been subjected to multiple treatments. If the direct model works anywhere, it should produce longitudinal gains in student learning resulting from both campuses' years of development around these complex learning goals.

In the case of WSU's Critical Thinking Project, data from 1999 to 2003 already documented short-term gains in student's levels of critical thinking when their teachers adapted courses to improve the ways they addressed that outcome. Sample assignments from fifty faculty who had participated in the earlier Critical Thinking Project, along with interviews of those faculty, characterized the staying power of their learning from that project.

Equally positive results regarding student learning were obtained by training a set of critical thinking raters and conducting rating sessions with the recent student work samples the faculty had provided. Each faculty member provided a class set of samples, together with the assignments to which the students had responded. Raters assessed a randomly selected one-third of that total (n=429 WSU student work products). In addition, the rating sessions included student work samples from Carleton (more on that below). As described above, students from 1999 to 2003 demonstrated an overall

TABLE 6.1. AVERAGE WASHINGTON STATE UNIVERSITY CRITICAL THINKING (CT) RATINGS BY FACULTY PARTICIPATION RATES

	LOW PARTICIPATING (2.2 EVENTS)	HIGH PARTICIPATING (1–3 ADDITIONAL EVENTS)	HIGH-PARTICIPATING (MORE THAN 3 ADDITIONAL EVENTS)
Average CT scoring for assignments	2.8	3.7	4.2
Average CT scoring on student work samples	2.6	3.6	4.1

average improvement of 0.7 points (on a six-point scale) in sections of a course in which the instructor used the critical thinking methodology, as compared to students in sections where the instructor had not undergone that faculty development experience. The treatment group in a first-year course scored an average of 3.1. The treatment group in a senior-level course scored 3.4. However, samples collected in 2009–2010, from a mixed group of lower- and upper-division students, produced an increase in average score to 4.1 for students in high-participating faculty members' classes (see table 6.1). In other words, as faculty continued to refine and develop their pedagogies for teaching critical thinking, students' learning outcomes demonstrated further increases in the level of student performance on that set of outcomes.

In addition to rating the samples, raters also measured the extent to which the assignments asked for critical thinking (again, on a six-point scale). As table 6.1 reveals, student scores track that level fairly closely, indicating a close match between the outcomes that course assignments identify and the outcomes that students develop. The results also clearly demonstrate that faculty development can matter to students' learning. Even a small amount of development (1–3 additional events per year) resulted in significant gains over the low-participating faculty members' students.

Some readers may object to these conclusions, claiming that of course students will do whatever faculty ask them to do. What happens when work from classes where faculty are not asking specifically for critical thinking is measured for critical thinking? On the one hand, this objection seems misplaced. Good teaching involves setting a high standard and then creating a series of tasks that help students meet that standard. Thus, all teachers ask students for specific outcomes, and students either deliver those outcomes or do not. If teachers are not clearly asking for an outcome (as is the case for the low-participators' assignments), then students will not display that outcome as clearly in their work. However, the work samples collected from WAC faculty and Junior Portfolio raters who had *not* participated in the Critical Thinking Project

**TABLE 6.2. COMPARISON OF LOW AND HIGH PARTICIPATORS
(OTHER THAN CT PARTICIPANTS)**

	LOW PARTICIPATING (2.2 EVENTS)	WAC WORKSHOP PARTICIPANTS	PORTFOLIO RATERS
Average CT scoring for assignments	2.8	3.4	3.6
Average CT scoring on student work samples	2.6	3.3	3.3
	N=20 faculty N=50 student samples	N=35 faculty N=100 student samples	N=27 faculty N=100 student samples

also confirm that complex outcomes like critical thinking are in fact addressed by faculty who are high participators in their development as teachers. Table 6.2 compares low-participating faculty with WAC faculty and portfolio raters. Note that all fifty WAC faculty and all forty portfolio raters qualified as high-participating faculty.

None of the faculty in these samples were trained on the critical thinking teaching methods—hence the lower sample size, because WAC faculty and portfolio raters who had participated in the Critical Thinking Project were eliminated. While none of the assignments approached the level of assignments from Critical Thinking Project faculty (see table 6.3), they did more explicitly ask for critical thinking than did the low-participating faculty, and their students responded with average critical thinking scores that were higher than those from students in low-participating faculty members' classes. One can conclude that larger, complex learning outcomes tend to overlap, so that learning about building better writing assignments—whether that learning is formal (WAC workshop) or part of a routine event (reading student portfolios)—also helps faculty make students understand that good writing involves critical thinking. Thus, faculty development centered on a complex outcome helps students learn that outcome, but it also helps them address other outcomes.

Data from faculty assignments also revealed that Critical Thinking faculty had continued to innovate, another demonstration of the persistence and spread of effect described earlier.

The data on student learning also reveals matters of concern—in WSU's case, concern over the conditions under which contingent faculty work. Most adjunct and temporary faculty practiced what the researchers came to identify as "defensive" faculty development: they felt the need to participate in a very large number of development opportunities (some as many as twenty per year) so that their appointments would be

TABLE 6.3. AVERAGE WASHINGTON STATE UNIVERSITY
CRITICAL THINKING (CT) RATINGS BY APPOINTMENT TYPE

	ADJUNCT (TERM-TO-TERM)	TEMPORARY (YEAR-TO-YEAR)	TENURE-TRACK
Average CT scoring for assignments	3.7	3.9	4.3
Average CT scoring on student work samples	3.4	4.1	4.4

renewed. While that need stimulated participation, it was paired with an avowedly cautious approach to experimentation in the classroom, lest student course evaluations go down.

Tenure-track faculty attended fewer department- or program-sponsored events, primarily because they teach a different set of courses. While temporary and adjunct faculty attended at least eight events a year, and some—the English 101 teachers—as many as twenty, no tenure-track faculty member reported more than eight. Still, the tenured faculty were far more willing to experiment with new assignments or techniques, since they did not have to worry about a temporary dip in course evaluations. Thus, for that set of high-participating faculty, higher critical-thinking scores result from the extra freedom to experiment.

It is worth remembering that the year-to-year temporary faculty were equally credentialed (PhD-level teachers) and in many cases far more experienced in teaching than most of the tenure-track faculty. Overall, then, differentials in outcomes can be attributed more to conditions of employment than to initial qualifications or subsequent teaching experience. And since the temporary faculty participated far more heavily in faculty development, they actually held an advantage over tenure-track faculty in opportunities for faculty learning. One might expect that their assignments would rate higher on asking for critical thinking and that their students would score at least as high on that outcome. Not so.

Comparing interview comments from temporary faculty and tenure-track faculty further reveals the ways that appointment types influence classroom innovation (see table 6.4).

More faculty development focused directly on improving teaching and learning results in higher performances from students, no matter what kind of appointment the teacher held. Still, faculty status matters, not so much because of qualifications but because of job security. Faculty whose positions are secure more readily incorporate what they learn from faculty-development opportunities into their teaching

TABLE 6.4. INTERVIEW COMMENTS FROM TEMPORARY
AND TENURE-TRACK FACULTY

TEMPORARY FACULTY	TENURE-TRACK FACULTY
I go to a lot of workshops and meetings, and I'm always learning more about how to teach better.	I probably attend 2–3 workshops of some kind each year. I think they are worthwhile because I put some of those ideas into practice.
If I'm going to try something new, I have to be pretty sure it'll work—or at least that it won't blow up in my face.	I like trying new techniques and assignments.
My annual reviews focus on my teaching evaluations, so I have to be careful to keep those up.	My department values my teaching, but I'm not sure the university really does.
I usually find someone who's tried stuff and talk with them about how to make it work before I put in on my syllabus.	I throw in a new assignment or two every so often, and if it works, I keep it. I'm always tinkering.

practices, and that freedom to experiment adds up to more learning for students. Putting teaching and learning under this kind of microscope yields more than just the expected results; it also provides information that might help improve teaching and learning in other ways. In this case, institutions can address the status of temporary faculty. Clearly, greater appointment security—whether tenure-track lines or longer continuing appointments—results in higher learning for students. While this sample did not allow for the comparison, further research might compare results from faculty on three-year (or longer) appointments and clinical faculty appointees with those from tenure-track faculty to see whether holding tenure is the key factor in these results, or whether other kinds of employment security would do just as well. Either way, robust faculty development, complete with well-designed evaluation, again yields more for the money, further justifying the expenditure.

The members of the Critical Thinking program conceived the project as a long-term effort, and they developed a strong research design—one that faculty in most disciplines could understand and appreciate. The mixture of quantitative and qualitative methods attracted the endorsement and the participation of faculty in the social sciences, the natural sciences, and the applied sciences, as well as the humanities faculty, whose disciplinary epistemologies made them less difficult to recruit to teaching-focused events. The collaborators also employed a measurement tool—the WSU Guide to Rating Critical Thinking—that they had carefully developed, defined, and broadly validated, and that could be applied to existing student work products from WSU classes. The ability to use student course work allowed the project to collect a very large data set and to track change over time in a highly reliable fashion. The Critical Thinking Project was also able to disseminate its results in multiple ways, from direct feedback to individual faculty participants to large-scale reports to the WSU community and beyond. At a research university, a teaching and learning project that results in substantial conference presentations and publications—not to mention a prestigious FIPSE grant—earns the kind of credibility that attracts more and more faculty participants. All these factors stand behind the Tracer Project's ability to collect its data and to produce results, even a decade later.

The Carleton Version: QuIRK and Critical Thinking

Carleton's several attempts to engage faculty with the WSU Guide to Rating Critical Thinking demonstrate the difficulty of transplanting even a successful initiative from one campus to another. Carleton's students as a whole arrive on campus better prepared for college study in measurable ways compared to WSU's first-year students. While the WSU Guide was successfully adapted for a targeted study of genomics learning in biology courses, general interest in the instrument was lacking. Carleton faculty remained concerned with students' thinking and reasoning competencies, but that concern was more specific than at WSU. For example, a group of faculty arose who were interested particularly in quantitative reasoning. Instead of approaching this concern with the WSU Guide, this group sampled Carleton's writing portfolios to assess whether students were using quantitative reasoning and found that if an assignment asked explicitly for quantitative reasoning, students responded; but if the assignment did not specifically cue for quantitative reasoning, students rarely used quantitative evidence to support and clarify their assertions.

Based on that survey of portfolios, the faculty group won a FIPSE grant to promote a faculty initiative on Quantitative Inquiry, Reasoning, and Knowledge (QuIRK). The group aimed for the kind of quantitative analyses that WSU's Critical Thinking Project had achieved, but the initiative began by identifying ways of infusing QuIRK into Carleton's curriculum and into its faculty development initiatives. A QuIRK rubric was used in surveys of portfolios in subsequent years, revealing an increase in the frequency of QuIRK in students' writing but then a leveling off, though the reason for the plateau remains unclear. Despite the quantitative leveling, qualitative results—data gathered from faculty and students about the effectiveness of QuIRK assignments in promoting more highly valued learning experiences—were sufficient both to identify next steps and to build a QuIRK requirement into Carleton's new curriculum, as well as to establish QuIRK as an emphasis in faculty development. In coming years, then, QuIRK may achieve more robust analyses of students' learning outcomes. Nonetheless, the project was able to document an increase in the frequency with which faculty were asking students to perform QuIRK, as well as an even greater incidence of QuIRK in students' written products. These are significant learning gains.

At Carleton College, the WAC program's alliance with QuIRK emphasizes the rhetorical uses of data, broadening the agendas of workshops, summer grant possibilities, and portfolio assessment. Therefore, in addition to a faculty curriculum devoted to assignment design, classroom strategies such as peer review, sequenced assignments, the use of drafts, and formative response to drafts, WAC/QuIRK addressed responsible uses of numbers. The QuIRK program for faculty has focused on two primary applications: to use numbers accurately and meaningfully within a quantitative argument or to set the context for a piece of writing that is not primarily quantitative but would benefit from some statistics, dates, and data. Initially, the Tracer group had hoped to perform quantitative analyses in testing QuIRK's impacts on faculty learning and student learning. As it became apparent that the QuIRK student work sampling and ratings would not align as well with the Tracer Project goals, the group turned to WSU's Guide as a tool that might at least reveal whether QuIRK was affecting students' higher-order thinking abilities in a more general way.

Interviews, observations, and other methods produced case studies from faculty members of first-year seminars, showing substantial rethinking and revision of specific learning goals and associated assignments over time, including specific attention to QuIRK. The Tracer team collected assignments and student work from these courses and found indications that the goals of faculty development were indeed reflected in the assignments themselves as well as in the student work—even for first-term, first-year students. However, these data were more exploratory findings than solid results. The team sought a way to place the evidence before readers outside of the project members, and a critical thinking rating session scheduled at WSU offered that opportunity. If the Critical Thinking Rubric was sensitive enough to surface the changes observed at Carleton, the rubric could be further adapted to serve local purposes—as had been the case in departments and programs at WSU.

Raters at WSU were willing to include student work outside of their institution, and a Carleton researcher looked forward to reading student writing from WSU as well, noting the benefits and limits of the Critical Thinking Rubric as well as the training process for raters. In addition, the WSU sample spanned more class years and disciplines than the five first-year seminars in the Carleton sample—a useful broadening of the reading context for all parties.

Carleton brought student writing samples (n=99) to two of the WSU rating sessions, and the results indicated an alignment between students' learning and faculty development around QuIRK and critical thinking. Student work from the first-year seminars (n=63) showed higher critical thinking ratings in three categories ("identifying a problem or issue," "supporting their position with data or evidence," and "communication") that aligned well with WAC and QuIRK outcomes. The lowest critical thinking rating scores for student work occurred on aspects not emphasized by the WAC and QuIRK faculty development (e.g., "develop own position or hypothesis" and "integrate other perspectives").

Confirming the effects of Carleton's development efforts, Carleton assignments rated the strongest on three features: "supporting their position with data or evidence," "identifying a problem or issue," and "identifying and considering the influence of context and assumptions." In both rating sessions—the second including work from senior-level classes—the three dimensions of the Critical Thinking Rubric that aligned best with Carleton faculty development showed higher scores across all student samples. Senior-level work scored even more highly across the three strong dimensions, suggesting that instruction in QuIRK and writing accumulates throughout the curriculum, producing continued learning. The small sample of senior work (n=5) must be viewed with caution, yet the results suggest further exploration.

Despite encouraging results from the critical thinking rating sessions at WSU, the Carleton team sought better evidence that would compare goals of faculty development at Carleton with student learning outcomes in critical thinking. Thus, they decided to develop a tool that more clearly matched the goals with changes in faculty practice and in students' learning.

Carleton researchers developed a comparison rubric (appendix 4) to identify individual improvement by rating dimensions of assignment prompts and student writing samples. Raters would be asked to compare a pair of assignment prompts or student writing samples along these dimensions on a scale to identify which of the pair was "better." The Carleton researchers were interested in pairing (1) earlier and later prompts written by the same faculty member and (2) student work written for earlier versions of assignments to work written for later versions of the assignment. This multi-dimensional rubric aligned with Carleton's faculty development goals. Raters used the rubric to compare two student work samples from the same assignment or two assignment prompts of similar nature in order to determine which paper and assignment prompt best fit the faculty development goals. These direct comparisons of two papers or two prompts on specific analytic measures related to faculty development goals allowed the team to detect changes that the Critical Thinking Rubric's more holistic instrument did not register.

Analysis of the assignment prompt ratings revealed that the new instrument was sensitive to Carleton's faculty development effects. Although ratings were not overwhelmingly skewed toward the newer assignments and papers from high participators' classes (e.g., "greatly better" or a rating of "3"), ratings were consistently higher along the dimensions of the rubric for these samples (see table 6.5). With this new rubric in mind, the Tracer team sampled for assignment prompts using the two distinct groupings: (1) earlier writing assignments from lower-participating faculty paired with comparable writing assignments from recent courses taught by higher-participating faculty, and (2) a revision sample consisting of pairs of earlier and later versions of the same assignment from faculty with a range of faculty development participation levels and disciplines. In examining assignments from this first sample—seventeen of twenty final determination ratings between the high- (more recent) versus lower-

TABLE 6.5. COMPARISON OF RUBRICS FOR STUDENT WORK SAMPLES AND COURSE ASSIGNMENTS

CC STUDENT WRITING RUBRIC	CC FACULTY ASSIGNMENT RUBRIC

• Demonstrates communication through clear language, effective writing mechanics, and strong organization
• Develops and presents an argument, hypothesis, or position
• Demonstrates a clear sense of the intended audience through literary devices, presentation of data, or voice
• Supports argument with appropriate data/evidence (includes citations)
• Uses precise language when addressing quantitative argument or data (avoids weasel words)
• Differentiates correlation from causation
• Makes use of visual representations within the text
• Identifies and assesses conclusions, implications, and consequences
• Demonstrates higher level thinking in terms of analysis, synthesis, integrative, or evaluative thinking
• Argues the student's own point of view
	• Provides opportunity to develop earlier assignments into a final product
	• Provides opportunity for feedback and revision
	• Gives guidelines for grading that are clearly articulated (and for acceptable writing)
	• Articulates learning goals of the assignment clearly
	• Elicits higher order thinking and writing
	• *For example*:
	  • Asks student to develop an argument, hypothesis, or position
	  • Requires student to write with a particular audience in mind
	  • Asks student to identify and assess conclusions, implications, and consequences
	• Prompts for effective use of data/evidence or quantitative reasoning
	• Prompts for effective use of visuals
	• Requires students to differentiate correlation from causation

(and earlier) participating faculty assignment prompts—the high participators' work was rated "better" in terms of alignment with faculty development goals. For the revision sample, raters selected the newer version of the assignment as better in ten of the twelve pairs sampled.

Ratings on individual elements showed that on average, the more recent and high participators' assignments were rated "better" than those from older and lower participators in prompting students to support their writing with effective data or other forms of evidence, featuring clearly stated grading guidelines, the learning goals, and the requirement for students to use effective visual material in their writing. Conclusion: faculty members (as represented in the samples) are including more WAC/QuIRK-promoted practices in newer assignment prompts than earlier efforts. This finding applies to both high and low participators, though high participators' assignments rated higher.

The ratings on students' papers also displayed improvement, though less conclusively than the assignments. Of the twenty-eight paper pairs from faculty members with a range of faculty development participation, raters identified sixteen newer student papers (57 percent) from higher-participating faculty members as holistically "better" in the forced-choice comparison. Given the discovery that all faculty, including low participators, are producing assignments that exhibit outcomes and methods promoted in faculty development, this proportion suggests that students in high-participators' classes do perform better. The full set of findings and a description of these rating sessions are reported in Willett et al. (2014).

Of the three high participators, Professor Hogan (not her real name) provides results that most closely met the researchers' expectations. Professor Hogan is a high WAC/QuIRK participant and leader who reported changing her teaching in response to faculty development participation. Faculty raters in the paired-comparison analysis found Professor Hogan's newer assignment better in providing students with clear guidelines, higher-order thinking, requiring appropriate data/evidence, and in providing students with opportunities for feedback.

These raters then assessed her newer student work as better than older samples. Raters agreed that newer papers were generally better, in four elements: argument, conclusions, higher-order thinking, and student point of view. The first three of these dimensions feature prominently in faculty development discussions at Carleton and reflect the researchers' own assessment of changes in the work over time, particularly in terms of higher-level thinking, and represent Professor Hogan's student learning goals.

Overall, more recently revised faculty assignment prompts rated higher than the older versions, suggesting the impact of faculty development. One difficulty with the forced comparison method, however, reflects the length of time Carleton has been pursuing a well-coordinated faculty development program. Thus, older versions of assignments already addressed common outcomes and employed commonly valued pedagogies. Therefore, the fact that most assignments rated only slightly better is probably an artifact of long-time high participation. Similarly, the fact that student samples also rated only slightly better than older samples may be because the older samples were written to assignments that had already shown the effects of earlier faculty development.

For example, Professors Sweet and Basil (pseudonyms) have the same levels of participation in faculty development as Professor Hogan, raising the expectation of similar improvement in assignments and student writing for their more recent students' work. This expectation was met in some instances, but in most, the more recent students performed at the "a little better" mark. However, newer student writing was somewhat better in terms of argument, conclusions, and higher-order thinking, which corresponds with the teachers' self-reported changes in teaching.[1] Thus, the paired-comparison rubric was able to identify quite fine-grained improvements in newer student writing: slight, but present, despite the fact that these faculty have been high participators for many years.

Finally, the Tracer team searched for some spread of faculty development effects in even the low-participator case, Professor Perkins (pseudonym). Interview and observational data showed widespread discourse among faculty and thinking about learning beyond individual faculty development activities. Perhaps, then, low participators' assignments and students' outcomes would show some impact from widespread faculty development efforts. Professor Perkins's newer students instead demonstrated poorer ratings for communication and higher-order thinking. Newer students' papers were rated better than older students' in terms of correlation versus causation (a QuIRK element) and in presenting their own point of view (not a WAC or QuIRK element). No student ratings even reached the "a little better" mark, despite Professor Perkins's discussions about QuIRK with the interviewer. The data show that low participators' assignments display some characteristics in common with Carleton's faculty development priorities, but the assignments are not sufficiently specific or do not change enough over time to provide students with a learning opportunity that could demonstrate positive differences.

The Tracer team hypothesized that WAC and QuIRK programming should result in differences between student writing based on (1) instructors' level of faculty development participation; (2) instructors' reported changes in their teaching; or (3) the period of time in which the instructors taught their class (e.g., before or after the college introduced WAC/QuIRK faculty development program activities). The paired-comparison approach helped the team identify more specific differences between pairs of papers and assignment prompts than did WSU's Critical Thinking Rubric.

As expected, the analytic breakdown that the paired comparison allows, as well as case-by-case analysis, shows areas of improvement that a purely holistic judgment may hide. Prominent in both the paper and assignment prompt ratings was the emphasis on evidence and argument, which are key areas of WAC and QuIRK faculty development. Results of the paired comparisons suggest that faculty do learn from and employ pedagogical techniques offered through formal faculty development.

The concomitant effects for student learning, while less clear, are worth pursuing. Over time, refinements in the comparison rubrics and in rating procedures can yield clearer results. The procedure highlights the need for longitudinal research on the same students. These samples compared lower-division work samples with upper-division ones, but not from the same students. A longitudinal study could focus on a single set of students and their learning experiences, yielding results on gains occurring from multiple exposures. Still, this first round at least provided evidence that when faculty learn better teaching methods, student learning also improves.

Writing Across the Curriculum at Both Institutions

Table 6.4 reveals that WSU faculty who have attended at least one WAC workshop create assignments that rate more highly on the critical thinking assignment inventory, and that their students' work also rates more highly in the critical thinking rating sessions. Those data confirm that when faculty learn to construct better writing assignments and/or when faculty revise courses so that they do a better job of supporting students' improving their writing, then students actually do write better—at least from the standpoint of the thinking exhibited in their papers. Since the faculty in this group had not also participated in the Critical Thinking Project, the data also indicate that when faculty work on promoting one important outcome (writing/communication), they often improve in promoting another (critical thinking). Furthermore, students from WAC faculty's classes clearly outperformed students from low-participating faculty members' classes, further confirming the usefulness of the WAC workshop. While writing and critical thinking are not necessarily related competencies (Condon and Kelly-Riley 2004), WAC workshops often address ways faculty assignments can elicit better thinking, as well as better writing, especially when the same faculty developers who ran the Critical Thinking Project also facilitate the WAC workshops. In this case—critical thinking and WAC—WSU's context resembles Carleton's because of the overlap between two important learning outcomes. Each lends efficacy to the other, and the real beneficiaries are the students, whose improved learning outcomes establish the usefulness of the original faculty development.

Another indication that students' writing experiences are better in courses taught by faculty who have undergone a learning process of their own with regard to assigning writing is that students in WAC faculty members' classes choose papers from those classes for their Sophomore Writing Portfolios. Rutz and Lauer-Glebov (2005) established at Carleton that the likelihood that a student would choose a paper from a given faculty member's course for the student's writing portfolio was in direct proportion to the number of faculty development events the faculty member had attended. In effect, students endorse their teachers' learning by voting with their papers. This kind of endorsement holds true for students at WSU as well. Of the fifty WAC workshop attendees interviewed at WSU, thirty-four taught courses in the lower division, and all required at least one written assignment in their lower-division classes. All those faculty signed off on at least one student's paper for the Junior Writing Portfolio—one hundred percent participation. Of the twenty low-participating faculty subjects—none of whom had attended a WAC workshop—sixteen regularly taught courses in the lower division. Eight of the sixteen required at least one written assignment in those courses. Of the eight, none had signed off on even one paper for a student's writing portfolio. Thus, faculty development in WAC results in writing experiences that students value and are willing to rely on when the quality of their writing is at stake.

Carleton's data from WAC confirm these findings, even though at Carleton, faculty development is sufficiently robust that separating out WAC effects from other outcomes is impossible. Still, the comparison ratings described above for detecting change in students' critical thinking competencies also reveal the learning effects of WAC on students' achievements in writing. The paired-comparison assignment rubric matched teaching practices to desired learning outcomes from the student writing rubric. For example, comparing recent faculty assignments and student responses with earlier ones, the rating sought to identify the effects of the WAC-promoted practice of backward design and "scaffolding" of assignments in both the assignments and students' writing. In this approach, faculty create their course beginning with their expectations for what students should know and be able to do at the end of the course. They then design assignments that will build upon one another and help students reach these goals. The ratings revealed this approach as it was represented in faculty assignment prompts through references to earlier or later assignments (e.g., "provides opportunity to develop earlier assignments into a final product"). In addition, rating pairs of student papers provided evidence of better student writing in more recent courses. These writing improvements are exemplified by more polished, clear writing or by higher levels of analysis, synthesis, and evaluation (for most of the student writing rubric items), depending on the course's goals.

A look at Professor Hogan's assignments shows that she revised an earlier assignment in several significant ways, most of which are more oriented to her learning in WAC development events than in others:

- scaffolding assignments in course design
- providing early opportunities for feedback on writing
- providing opportunities for writing revision
- providing clear expectations and use of a grading rubric
- employing peer review of writing in the classroom
- developing students' QuIRK skills (how to find, use, analyze, and evaluate quantitative data)

The first five of the six changes Professor Hogan discussed relate to writing, while the sixth pertains to QuIRK. Comparisons of her earlier assignments with more recent ones revealed that the more recent assignments were indeed more evocative of established WAC practices at Carleton. Raters then assessed work from Professor Hogan's more recent students as better than samples from less recent students, who responded to the earlier assignment. Raters agreed that newer papers were better, in general, on four elements: argument, conclusions, higher-order thinking, and student point of view—and three of these four dimensions reflect Professor Hogan's learning in WAC faculty development. These analyses are consistent throughout the data: faculty attend WAC development events. As a result, faculty change their assignments—sometimes radically, but more often, as in Stevens's case, in more of an evolutionary pattern, reflecting the faculty member's continuing learning process, rather than a "conversion" pattern. In response, student writing samples display improved performances on the newer assignments.

Writing Portfolios and Student Learning Outcomes

Again, table 6.4 shows that critical thinking performance in students papers from WSU portfolio raters' courses was higher than in low-participating faculty members' students and even than in papers from courses taught by WAC faculty—despite the fact that the sample excluded portfolio raters who had attended a WAC workshop or who had participated in the Critical Thinking Project. A routine development activity of rating writing portfolios leads raters to make changes in their own teaching practices. Table 6.4 reveals that, as a result, students' performances in critical thinking are rated significantly higher than performances from classes taught by low participators.

The addition of QuIRK and other curricular initiatives results in mixed influences on students' learning, so the specific effects of WAC programming has become more difficult to isolate. The resulting problem—a nice one to have—is a collage of overlapping, interactive faculty development opportunities that seem to affect teaching and learning in combination.

Developing an Action Agenda: A Continuation

Overall, this research confirms that the effects of faculty development do include improvements in student learning outcomes. While the Tracer Project limited its scope to two institutions and to the outcomes those institutions have prioritized in common, nevertheless, various kinds of faculty development—including some activities that are not overtly designed as faculty development—do result in changes in teaching practices that generate corresponding changes in student learning, as demonstrated in actual student work products. Detecting student learning is not difficult. Tying it, among all the possible influences, to faculty development is difficult, but not impossible.

In order to achieve the connection, development initiatives must design research methods into their processes, whether those are individual workshops or long-term initiatives. Such designs must collect data in ways that isolate as much as possible the effects of faculty learning on student learning, and that triangulate with each other to confirm or contradict each method's findings. Few institutions will begin with the set of resources that Carleton and WSU did, given these institutions' prior efforts at faculty development and the substantial data set represented in the writing portfolios at each place. Still, any institution can begin collecting samples of student learning—most have done so already as part of an accreditation self-study, if for no other reason—and of faculty's teaching materials. Then, using materials and methods at hand, any institution can make a beginning—and from there it can design ways to collect faculty learning outcomes and student learning outcomes so that they match up to reveal any effects.

The key variables, as noted above, are (1) the type of faculty development to be studied, (2) the methods used, and (3) the assessment instrument applied to relevant data. For the first, institutions must promote the learning outcomes that faculty value. Typically, those will begin with broader outcomes such as writing, higher-order thinking, information literacy, and quantitative reasoning—the outcomes that tend to show up in most institutions' goals for the baccalaureate. Beginning with one or two that are most highly valued is wise, since that ensures broad participation—and, therefore, widespread effects on student learning. As time passes, those values will evolve, as the data in this study show. Thus, the faculty development evaluation process has to keep track of faculty values about student learning outcomes and broaden the focus of development initiatives to address their evolution.

Perhaps, if nothing else, this chapter dispels the long-standing assumption that such effects are so difficult to identify that the effort should not be made. Mixed methods and a willingness to begin with what one has and build over time yield results that faculty across campus can believe. Perhaps the one best first step is to establish a baseline for future data—just collect assignments, syllabi, and student work products—and move forward, keeping track along the way.

Given the data presented in chapters 4–6, the connection between changes faculty make in their assignments and changes in students' learning outcomes is clear. When faculty improve their teaching methods—or merely improve an assignment—improvement in student learning is detectable. To be fair, one should point out that, given these connections, the process would work the other way, too. Changes for the worse in faculty practices would therefore produce negative effects on students' learning. Thus, mounting serious faculty development efforts is even more crucial to an institution's effectiveness as a place for higher learning. Well-designed faculty development definitely yields great value—more and more so when the development efforts are so coordinated as to encourage a productive culture of teaching and learning on campus.

In the end, what does success look like? It will look different depending on institutional context, so to some extent success must be defined by the institution's developing the methods to discover the connections. These two campuses reveal two probably common models: a centralized initiative and a distributive model that develops synergies among a variety of individual initiatives. WSU's Critical Thinking Project was organized centrally, supported by a large grant, and attracted faculty because they shared the central value of the Project—promoting critical thinking in the classroom. The outlines of that model are already evident in the WAC programs at many institutions, so this is certainly one pattern for successful outcomes.

Carleton's more distributed model, which began with the portfolio as an agent of faculty development around writing, provides another model more common in smaller institutions where a sense of "community of the whole" helps an initiative gain momentum, and where the transparency of results is easier to achieve. Perhaps one might respond to these models because they are most familiar. The Tracer Project does not offer them as definitive, but as illustrative—and Tracer researchers look forward to seeing other models at work as other institutions pursue this line of research.

7 Faculty Development Matters

LEARNING IS BOTH an individual and a collective activity. For faculty members, a spiral of learning lasts their entire careers, drawing on the lessons learned in their own teaching, from interactions with others, and from professional development—formal, self-directed, and resulting from routine campus activities. That learning is situated in and dependent on the context for learning in the institution. That context is changing as the campus leadership and faculty collectively participate in a spiral of learning that encompasses both understanding more about how teaching and learning work on campus and how to increase their collective ability to improve that understanding. Student learning occupies a third spiral as individual students learn in interaction with the students and faculty around them. This chapter focuses on the importance of these interactions and strategies for maximizing the learning taking place at all levels on campus.

Broadly speaking, faculty development has measurable impacts on teaching. Existing research and the current project confirm that faculty consistently self-report learning gains aligned with workshop goals at the end of these experiences. Tracer Project interviews demonstrate that faculty can look back at workshops in their past and describe changes in their teaching aligned with these goals. Further, an analysis of these subjects' syllabi, assignments, methods, and grading scales verifies that their instruction has changed as they claimed it had. Just as significant a finding is that these impacts are cumulative. Participants who amass a more extensive faculty development history—for example, participating in the extensive Critical Thinking Project treatment—show measurably larger changes in their teaching than faculty whose participation is slight, such as a single departmental workshop on the same topic. These results hold true at both Carleton and WSU, though the pathways to change differ widely at the two institutions. The effects can be measured using the WSU Guide to Rating Critical Thinking or by developing a comparative methodology such as the Haswell rating scheme used in this study at Carleton. In short, formal faculty development produces measurable changes in the way participants teach.

In addition, faculty development experiences that stem from self-directed improvement efforts or even routine events that are not aimed at improving teaching matter as well, and almost as much as formal development, probably because faculty engage in their own development as teachers over time, in recurring contexts ranging from rating portfolios, to evaluating colleagues' performance in class or being evaluated themselves, to participating in departmental efforts to reform curricula for majors and evaluate the results of those changes. For instance, participants in portfolio readings at both institutions developed stronger assignments (as measured by the WSU Guide to Rating Critical Thinking and the Haswell comparison method at Carleton). Portfolio reading and other forms of curriculum development, program design, and assessment that engage groups of faculty in discussing teaching and learning are an important and heretofore overlooked form of faculty development that has direct impact on teaching. Faculty engaged in communal scoring of student work reflect on their experiences with students and then modify their teaching to obtain the behaviors valued in these discussions. Furthermore, faculty engaged in discussions of learning goals or curriculum design also adopt or adapt methods that are valued in these discussions or practices that lead to valued learning outcomes. Faculty who undergo or carry out performance evaluations that focus on teaching carry away with them the stronger aspects of a colleague's performance or the benefits of a colleague's observations, therefore making changes to teaching materials that result in changes in their students' learning outcomes.

Just as important contextual and affective variables support or hinder student learning in particular classes, these variables also matter in the process of understanding the impact of professional development activities on teaching. Faculty are motivated to attend professional development activities for reasons that run from a critical problem in class to the desire for a free lunch. It should come as no surprise that those with strong internal motivation to change their teaching show larger changes in their teaching—but all participants show some changes, changes that matter in the classroom. Indeed, even faculty who did not attend a development event demonstrated some benefits from the event because of the spread of effect from such events.

Similarly, faculty with strong self-efficacy who perceive recommended changes in teaching as carrying little risk are more likely to make changes. Practice and support for implementation, as exemplified in the Critical Thinking Project at WSU, increase the self-efficacy of participants and promote changes in practice. Likewise, a culture that values experimentation and accepts the associated risk, as at Carleton or for tenured faculty at WSU, also improves self-efficacy and supports changes in practice. Finally, contextual variables, like the coincidence in time of the development experience and the creation or revision of an assignment that can make use of lessons learned, or a schedule that allows extra time for course development (perhaps through grant support), enhance the ability to make changes. All these factors, and more that are yet to be identified, contribute to making faculty development most effective for participants and most likely to drive improvements in students' learning.

This project confirms existing research that states or implies that faculty development produces changes in teaching. It also confirms the greater difficulty in demonstrating changes in students' learning that are directly attributable to changes in specific assignments or courses. Success in measuring the impact of the Critical Thinking Project on student learning at WSU led to formulating a best-case scenario for such measurements: (1) the treatment was longitudinal, with faculty participating in multiple workshops that engaged them in an iterative cycle of assignment development, feedback, and testing; (2) the treatment took place many years ago, allowing participants to refine their implementation through time; and (3) the instrument measuring changes in student learning was developed to specifically align with local professional development goals.

At Carleton, the Critical Thinking Rubric was less successful in detecting improvements in student learning, for reasons that involved the different kinds of students at the different institutions, as well as the divergent means for faculty development. Instead, pair-wise scoring of assignments using a rubric well aligned with professional development goals at Carleton proved more sensitive. In addition, the comparison methodology detected consistent but relatively small improvements in student scores, though the changes are aligned with professional development experience. These smaller improvements most likely result from the context of faculty development at Carleton, where development begins even before a faculty member is hired and continues throughout employment. Thus, any change in assignments or learning can only be measured since the last engagement in development, rather than in a before-and-after comparison. In both these cases, though, an analysis of student work through time for a faculty member who has been involved in a rich set of professional development activities for some number of years produced changes in teaching that match improvements in students' learning.

Several complications impact the ability to measure student learning gains associated with improved instruction. Early gains in critical thinking as one begins to construct arguments are large, but they become incrementally smaller and more difficult to measure as students gain experience. At WSU, for example, student work collected between 2000 and 2003 indicated that at first exposure to a critical thinking teaching methodology, students' average scores jumped by 1.1 points on a six-point scale. As a result of a second exposure in a later course, the additional average gain was 0.5 points. As exposures accumulated, gains shrank, until they leveled off between four- and six-course exposures. Thus, comparing gains from before exposure to after the sixth exposure yields strong results, while comparing gains between the second and third exposures demonstrates weaker gains. These context-related complications mean that short-term measurements are far less likely to provide evidence of change than are longer-term or cross-curricular measurements.

In addition, scores on a particular assignment are impacted heavily by variations in student ability, preparation, and understanding of content. Writing and critical thinking skills improve through ongoing instruction, feedback, and practice. Thus, scores on any particular assignment are greatly impacted by all of the students' prior instruction in writing and critical thinking. Since this is the case, the strongest indications of the impacts of faculty development on student learning will appear in institutional studies of learning over the course of an undergraduate degree. Work that demonstrates learning within degree programs or across institutions as part of accreditation self-studies moves in this direction. Learning instruments like the 2009 Guide to Rating Critical and Integrative Thinking enable research within and across institutions, though this project demonstrates that specific methodologies for tracking faculty and student learning require locally designed instruments and methods and need to be closely aligned with professional development goals to pick up the desired effects.

Several important conclusions from this work speak to those who wish to measure the efficacy of particular professional development programs. First, short timescales increase the difficulty of measuring impacts of professional development activities on student learning. Measures of student learning need to overcome the substantial noise in the signal, requiring laborious scoring of many pieces of work. Measures need to be customized for the specific professional development goals. Further, it takes time for faculty to incorporate and refine changes in teaching. Second, it may be easier to look for changes in faculty practice, motivation, and self-efficacy. Assignment analysis, both rubric-scored and comparative, proved a valuable way to demonstrate change that can be efficiently scaled. While not explored by this study, instruments that measure motivation to change and self-efficacy may also be efficient and compelling measures of impact. As further studies demonstrate the direct connections between faculty learning and student learning, the evidence will mount for pursuing the easier task—studying faculty learning and its impacts on course syllabi, assignments, grading methods, and so forth—rather than the more complicated and labor-intensive one of measuring changes in student learning over time and across the curriculum. In either case, such a study requires multiple methodologies, designed or tailored to fit the local context, and triangulated so that the data speak to each other.

All of the above results flow from data that verify the Direct Path, a model that connects faculty learning with changes in faculty practice and resulting changes in students' learning outcomes. However, Tracer Project data also show spread of effect far beyond the faculty member who attends a formal development event. The Context Model addresses ways that an institution's structure either promotes or hinders—or perhaps, in many ways, both promotes and hinders—the spread of effect described in earlier chapters. Attending to the flow of information throughout an institution helps answer the question of how faculty development might strengthen the culture of teaching and learning on a campus.

The Context Model offers a way of understanding how institutional resources devoted to faculty development can be leveraged to ensure the largest improvement in teaching and, in turn, student learning. Whereas institutional investment in faculty learning takes many forms, this study focused on specific learning opportunities offered through workshops and other formal occasions. In studying those events, the importance of self-directed learning on the part of faculty emerged as an important factor. Faculty work on their teaching even when formal faculty development events are inconvenient or unavailable. The entire history of the scholarship of teaching and learning demonstrates that infusing research methodologies into the self-development process amplifies the results, and Tracer data confirm that self-development also produces positive changes in students' learning. In short, the more intentional and methodical the self-development, the more likely it is to cause gains in students' learning.

Furthermore, the casual interactions among faculty, administrators, students, and others provide a fertile medium for the spread of teaching and learning ideas based on institutional values. A thriving faculty development program reaches faculty who may not attend personally but are themselves affected by their colleagues' experience through conversation, observation, evaluation for tenure and promotion, and other routine interactions within the institution. The closer these routine events are to the classroom or the curriculum, the more likely they are to affect the teaching practices of participants. Thus, WSU portfolio raters changed their teaching practices in response to observations they made in the process of scoring writing portfolios.

Tracer data demonstrated a connection between those changes and improved student performances. Specific changes in practice were harder to identify as an outcome of classroom observations, for example, or as a result of conversations in the hallway, but to the extent that the institution's pedagogical and curricular values are "in the air," such conversations do nonetheless contribute to individual faculty members' awareness of institutional expectations and therefore to the faculty member's practices.

Since all three sites for faculty development contribute to improving teaching, and since those contributions are amplified as more and more faculty adopt common values and employ signature pedagogies, institutions must learn to bring together formal professional development with an institutional culture that generates improved teaching and learning on campus.

Strategies for Success: What Will Make Professional Development Easier and More Effective?

Looking across the initiatives in the study, researchers identify several factors that are common when things work well. In a robust situation, faculty learning about teaching leads to improvements in students' learning practices and outcomes. The attempt to measure improvements in student learning—and particularly in response to specific initiatives in faculty development—can run into many obstacles, and that is perhaps one reason that so few such studies exist. Carleton has sponsored a broad range of faculty-led development initiatives. At WSU, where the size of the institution dictates a different model, successful cases arise when the units conducting faculty development focus their efforts on competencies that faculty value highly. Nearly all (98 percent) of WSU's Writing Across the Curriculum (WAC) faculty subjects and Critical Thinking alumni indicated that their most important reason for participating was that they saw writing and/or critical thinking as an important learning outcome for their students. The faculty wanted to know how better to teach toward that outcome. One can deduce, then, that a challenging case would result when a top-down initiative promotes an outcome that the faculty care little or nothing about, or when there is no consensus about the outcome being promoted.

The most successful initiatives at WSU and at Carleton are the ones that were backed by sufficient resources. Resources help in at least two ways. First, they indicate the seriousness of the effort. Carleton's strong funding of faculty development, from stipends to meals to mini-grants to institutional support for the Perlman Learning and Teaching Center to support for grant writing, all testify to the institution's seriousness about the effort. WSU is less willing to fund such efforts from its own resources, but one of the features that drew faculty to the Critical Thinking Project was funding from the Fund for Improvement of Post-Secondary Education (FIPSE). FIPSE grants are highly competitive and therefore seen as prestigious by faculty. That imprimatur helped faculty understand that the project was "real" and was worth joining. Further, the funds allowed the program to be fully staffed and well executed and for the faculty to be rewarded for their participation. From these indicators of success, one can deduce that a challenging case would be an initiative that did not enjoy overt support from the institution, or one that simply did not have the resources to deliver on its promises. On most campuses, the most important resource faculty have is their time, and when they detect that their investment of time and effort is not likely to pay off, then drawing them to an event will be difficult.

Successful programs at Carleton and at WSU were rendered easier because they began with data about student learning and employed a research-based methodology from the beginning that also aimed at the very least to discover more about students' learning. In establishing their writing portfolios, both institutions set out not just to measure students' writing competencies, but to gather data that would help their WAC programs improve those learning outcomes. And on both campuses, those research designs have produced significant publications (see, e.g., Haswell 2000 and 2001; Condon and Kelly-Riley 2004; Rutz and Lauer-Glebov 2005; Condon 2009), as well as significant grant-funded spinoff initiatives. Challenges, then, would come from poorly conceived initiatives that are incapable of producing their own positive outcomes and unlikely to act as models for further innovation. Within the context of higher education, credibility is most easily earned by ensuring a solid research design. Without that, success can be hard to come by.

Ambition is another factor that produces success, though it may operate counter-intuitively. Worthwhile learning goals such as the ones institutions choose for their baccalaureate outcomes are all complex goals and therefore difficult to measure: writing, critical or creative thinking, quantitative and symbolic reasoning, information literacy, self-actualization, civic engagement, and others are broad competencies that students will encounter in a range of course experiences, not in just one place in the curriculum. However, addressing such large, complex, and widespread outcomes makes a development initiative easier because faculty can see that their efforts will be worthwhile. Targeting simpler outcomes provides a clearer focus for development, but it also carries the message that this development is not really very important—thus making success more difficult to attain.

Pursuing an ambitious set of learning outcomes also means designing the project so that it offers multiple treatments and measures outcomes in both the short and long terms. For example, just as students do not learn everything they need to know about writing in one course, so faculty don't learn everything they need to know about using writing as a learning tool in their courses in one workshop. Indeed, faculty require multiple iterations for any innovation to become fully part of their practice. Thus, making change easier means providing support that continues over several iterations and that focuses on the change process itself, providing faculty with the tools to continue innovating long after a specific initiative is finished. Similarly, since faculty learning takes place over time, measurement of student learning outcomes must also occur over time. The data above demonstrate that immediate change can happen. The data also demonstrate that when faculty continue to innovate, student gains continue to increase. Short-term assessments fail to capture continued improvement. In other words, the means of measuring and evaluating faculty and student learning need to be congruent with the ambitious goals being measured. To the extent that this happens, the pathway to success is easier.

Designing an effort so that faculty participants have a role to play in shaping the initiative also helps ensure success. Faculty come into these projects with a wide range of expertise. Scientists, poets, engineers, teacher educators, librarians, orchard managers, accountants, veterinarians, nurses, philosophers, and more bring their attention to these outcomes, and if the project is open to their input along with their participation, they can help optimize the development so that it can benefit even more faculty—and their ideas for spreading the results can result in the kind of productive, generative culture of teaching and learning that is seen at Carleton and in more localized programs at WSU. Faculty like to participate, not merely attend, and they like the recognition that comes when the work they do becomes part of the project. The absence of this openness to participation is an event that allows information to flow in only one direction, from presenters to attendees. A one-way flow of information is no more effective in generating sustained learning in campus initiatives than in a classroom. Successful efforts engage faculty in learning and guiding sustained change.

Finally, measuring student learning will be easier if conducted on a longitudinal design. The critical thinking research at WSU was easier because of the presence of baseline data. The original project had collected "before" samples as well as "comparison" samples, so the Tracer Project inherited data from before any faculty development about critical thinking had taken place, as well as after the original project had ended. As a result, the study could compare the samples gathered at WSU in 2009–2010 with those earlier samples in order to know what changes might have occurred in the meantime. The Carleton ratings were more difficult both because there were no baseline data to speak of and because faculty development happens continuously, so that in comparing previous samples to current ones, researchers were tracking a faculty learning process that was gradual but continuous. Distinctions were present, but differences tended to be slight. Longitudinal data would track students from matriculation through graduation, so that as those students displayed advances in learning, those effects could be traced back into faculty practices that resulted from development initiatives (or other sources). In the absence of at least two sampling points, separated by a sufficient amount of time for learning to occur, differences are difficult if not impossible to determine.

Multiplying Impact: Creating a Generative Culture of Teaching and Learning

That every campus has a culture of teaching and learning is both an obvious statement and one that bears repeating. The key concern on any campus is to work with that culture to make it more productive, more effective in promoting best practices in the classroom. Looking carefully at common goals among the faculty, building a set of formal opportunities for development that is buttressed by a network of resources to support better teaching, and broadly sharing the outcomes of those efforts can go a long way toward increasing that culture's impact.

The data in this study demonstrate some of the differences between small institutions, where one can speak of a single culture of teaching and learning, and large ones, where one thinks in terms of multiple cultures of teaching and learning. The differences can be stark, but as the data show, there are common elements to consider. On both campuses, for example, faculty care deeply about teaching, and they work to improve their teaching. Even the most reluctant faculty members can see that being good teachers is in their enlightened self-interest. That self-interest explains the presence of a culture of teaching and learning.

Our work makes clear the importance of this culture in enhancing the spread of information and ideas about teaching and learning across campus and supporting the use of this information and these ideas in teaching. A generative culture multiplies the impact of formal faculty development, enhances self-motivated, individual faculty learning, and supports faculty experimentation in their courses. A generative culture creates an environment that promotes faculty learning so that faculty can encourage improvements in students' learning. Such a culture is founded on shared needs to improve student learning, is rich with opportunities to learn, and is self-reflective, studying the impact of individual and collective actions on teaching and learning.

Tracer Project data help identify several common elements that characterize a productive culture of teaching and learning. Institutions that place a widespread value on the importance of teaching—as shown by an ability of all faculty to discuss at a high level their own teaching and their own students' learning—have established a level of knowledge about teaching and an awareness of its importance. Getting to that point requires actions by the institution. Administration can supply strong support for improving teaching in the form of professional development programming, curriculum and course development grants, academic leave policies that support teaching as well as research proposals, and professional development planning processes that faculty lead, or that are at least responsive to faculty input about the directions such development initiatives should take.

Institutions can build on that foundation by infusing considerations of good teaching not only into professional development but into routine activities as well: hiring processes, initial and ongoing enculturation of new faculty, promotion and tenure procedures, provisions for revising and evaluating curriculum, and other occasions that may look more like logistical processes than occasions for developing good teaching. A generative culture also depends on a widespread understanding that teaching can be improved by learning from research and the experiences of others as shown by a scholarly attention to teaching. Initiatives related to curriculum and teaching need to be research-based and data-driven, in order to gain the respect of faculty researchers, pointing the way for further progress, and to carry greater weight in the public sector as well. Current assessment plans may perforce focus on institutional accountability or accreditation, but those processes must be designed as research projects so that they identify new initiatives, help generate curriculum redesign, foster community discussions of challenging topics, and lead to greater faculty participation in professional development. Flipping institutional assessment processes, so that the principal goals are to improve teaching and learning and the incidental goals are to provide data for accountability or accreditation, allows those processes to enrich a culture of teaching and learning on campus.

As a whole, the professional development program needs to foster innovation and to make clear the message that the institution as a whole fosters diversity of opportunity and curricular approach. On this level, effective practice engages faculty in learning about their own teaching and exploring the successes of others: talking with colleagues or reading the extensive research on the scholarship of teaching and learning. Depending on the discipline and the institution, research centered on teaching may or may not be highly valued, and may or may not be rewarded in departmental annual reviews or promotion and tenure processes. Those disciplines and institutions that place a lower value on research about teaching need to make changes. Overall, a campus must establish strong support for experimentation and risk-taking among all its faculty—tenure-track, non-tenure-track, or adjunct—so that the risks involved in making change in one's own classroom are reduced to the point that faculty can experiment with new teaching methods without risking their careers. Faculty want to emphasize good teaching, so when their positions are secure (once they have tenure), they will readily engage in improving their teaching. That desire needs institutional support in the form of faculty review processes that protect actions intended to improve teaching, of the ability to consult with colleagues or experts about planning for innovation or evaluating new practices, and of removing any other barriers the institution may have put in the way of faculty who seek to improve their classroom practices.

These factors provide a strong context for a generative culture of teaching and learning. Such a culture transforms a narrowly focused investment—say, for example, into better writing or critical thinking—into a set of practices that have a campus-wide positive impact on teaching and learning. Granted, these are not the only factors, but they are the ones suggested by the results of this study. While the data do not reveal which factors above or which items on the action agenda are more critical than others, collective experience leads us to identify the ones that seem to us the most likely starting points for generating a more productive culture of teaching and learning on any campus.

Reflecting on findings from both WSU and Carleton, the Tracer team identified features of a generative culture of teaching and learning and suggestions for ways to strengthen each aspect. In a generative culture:

- It is clear that working on teaching and improving student learning are highly valued activities and an acceptable use of faculty and staff time. Developing a generative culture of teaching and learning requires actions at all levels, bringing together administrative support and grassroots efforts. Actions can extend from administrative funding of professional development opportunities to faculty reaching out to discuss teaching and learning with colleagues old and new. Library staff, IT staff, students, and any others who are likely partners in the enterprise—not just support staff, but partners—should all be engaged, and incentives should be provided to those who pursue good teaching. Mini-grants for innovation or for scholarship on teaching and learning, innovator awards, and more can deliver the message that teaching matters in ways that are non-punitive. Rewarding the better teachers—and particularly the innovators—spurs the kind of energy that can make the culture more generative.
- Faculty are open to change and innovation in their teaching. This stance requires an atmosphere where such exploration is recognized and valued. Look for and promote people who are in the habit of continuous improvement. Develop tools to reflect on, learn about, and improve teaching. Some of those tools

involve looking at students' work to determine their responses to changes in teaching. Remove incentive barriers that prevent or slow down innovation in the classroom. Provide alternatives to student course evaluations so that when a course is under revision, faculty are rewarded for innovation; later on, the course can return to a performance format. Make faculty exchange of ideas an important part of the context, so that individuals making changes realize that they are not alone and so that successful changes spread among colleagues.

- There are abundant, diverse, and high-quality opportunities for learning about teaching and learning. Activities that are designed to engage faculty in learning and that support transformation of teaching are valued more highly by participants. While these can be provided at many levels, from individual departments to the entire institution, coordinated and/or funded opportunities indicate department or institutional support for a given initiative. Collegial opportunities to talk about teaching should be ubiquitous: lunches, book discussions, research forums, writing projects or support groups, outside lecturer events, small and large workshops: these are the kinds of opportunity for colleagues to make contact and trade ideas about good teaching.

- Gaining access to ideas about teaching is as easy as talking with the person in the next office. A generative culture of teaching and learning promotes a sense of community among faculty, staff, administrators, and students. The support structure for improving teaching goes beyond formal faculty development to embrace routine venues and to support individual faculty in their attempts to change. Build teaching into every possible administrative process. Make it prominent in curriculum reform, in annual reviews, and in promotion and tenure processes. Design the processes so that those doing the evaluation and those being evaluated have meaningful conversations about teaching. In any institutional processes that engage faculty—such as portfolio rating sessions and accreditation reviews—be sure a significant amount of attention is focused on effective teaching practices. Make the most of both formal and routine opportunities to promote good teaching.

- Support for innovation in teaching must come from both the top and the grassroots. Support from administrators who control financial resources is critical, while faculty, who are more aware of their own development needs, must be the primary impetus for innovation. The balance differs depending on the size of the institution and its prevailing culture of teaching and learning. Large institutions typically establish some sort of office of teaching and learning to lead development opportunities, and faculty development often occurs in a unit-by-unit pattern, while smaller schools tend to operate more as a single community.

- Institution-, college-, or department-wide initiatives all support innovation and change and reflect commonly held values and concerns. Stakeholders should identify and pursue opportunities for larger initiatives. WAC, QuIRK,

and Critical Thinking represent just a few of the overarching competencies
that faculty in every department or program value. Once faculty identify these
values, the institution can put its weight behind grant proposals that support
extended faculty development promoting those values—including assessments
that demonstrate the project's effectiveness.

As a culture of teaching and learning becomes more productive, it extends the
spread of effect among faculty within and across departments and colleges, as well as
among different institutions. Because faculty move from one institution to the next
or consult at other places, they embody possibilities for extending faculty learning
beyond the boundaries of a single department or college.

Recommendations for Jump-Starting a Generative Culture of Teaching and Learning: Supporting Faculty Learning about Teaching

This study began with the realization that faculty development is at risk because of
a lack of data demonstrating its effectiveness or its value to an institution. Like colleagues at many institutions, the researchers on the Tracer Project are themselves
faculty developers, in WAC, critical thinking, quantitative reasoning, portfolio evaluation, and the sciences. As such, faculty developers are continually called upon to
document the usefulness of our programming. Like so many others, the research
team focused on changes in faculty practice, assuming that as faculty improved their
teaching, students would benefit. That assumption is grounded in the widespread
practice among faculty developers of measuring effectiveness by the impact on faculty, and the evidence for such impact is clear and widespread. When faculty attend
formal development opportunities, engage in self-directed improvement processes,
or even undergo routine evaluations, faculty practices do change. The evidence is also
clear that even in the absence of formal faculty development, faculty spend a great
deal of time working on their teaching. These studies formed the foundation for the
Tracer Project.

However, knowing that faculty development impacts teaching is not enough.
The value of professional development experiences, and indeed of any strong move
to enhance faculty learning, rests on the ability to improve student learning, a primary goal and economic driver in academic institutions of all kinds. For that reason, research must produce data that can indicate whether and to what extent faculty
development initiatives added value to a college education in terms of improving students' learning, as represented in their actual classroom work products. At the end of
the Tracer study, the answer could not be clearer. When faculty improve their teaching, students learn more and their performance on course work improves. As greater
numbers of faculty make common cause of improving teaching, the goals of that
improvement tend to spread throughout the institution, and the likelihood of incorporating those goals as common values in routine administrative processes increases.

The conclusive piece in such work is devising ongoing means of measuring the effects of faculty development as they appear in student work products. Such a systematic approach demonstrates that faculty development adds value in measurable ways to the institution that invests in sound practices to help teachers address the challenges they face in their classrooms.

This work is made easier when realizing that many, most, if not all faculty care about their teaching. Tracer Project investigations indicate that large numbers of faculty are engaged in improving their teaching and participate in formal faculty development of some kind within their institution. This finding underscores other research that indicates the extent to which faculty put effort into improving their teaching practices, whether supported by formal faculty development or not. Much of the SoTL research consists of faculty designing and testing new ideas in the classroom, evaluating them with sound research methodologies current in their fields, and reporting on the results. Tracer results demonstrate the extent to which such work has penetrated the faculty at large, so that even at a large public university, the project could find no faculty who did not participate at all in faculty development, even though the low-participating faculty engaged at a minimal level. This confirmation refutes the widespread belief that college and university faculty care only about research and that they spend little time and effort on teaching. The Tracer Study found no evidence to support that common perception. The ability of faculty to focus on improving their teaching and their ability to bring new ideas and knowledge into practice depends on the institutional context. Thus, what many perceive as a failing of individual faculty to value teaching may in fact reflect the absence of a culture that supports teaching and learning.

Service work is often designed to support improved teaching, or does so implicitly; it therefore offers a plethora of under-utilized opportunities to support faculty efforts to improve their teaching. Portfolio rating sessions at both institutions, whether designed as faculty development opportunities or not, were powerful opportunities for learning about teaching. Raters offer more written assignments than their non-rater peers; those assignments are constructed in a more informed way; and students respond to raters' assignments with higher-rated performances. Furthermore, interviews at both institutions revealed the presence of many more possible opportunities for routine faculty development. The data support the recommendation that institutions pay careful attention to such events as hiring practices, faculty orientations, performance evaluations, curriculum planning, and many others as sites for conversations about good teaching practices.

The study's conclusions begin to illuminate the tremendous importance of professional development and a productive culture that supports teaching and learning. As strong as the conclusions are, they represent data from only two institutions: a large state-assisted land grant university and a small, elite, private liberal arts college. Would similar results emerge at other such institutions or at institutions of different types, including smaller state-assisted regional colleges, two-year colleges, or other kinds of institutions of higher education? Nothing in the results suggests that the results would differ, but nothing provides evidence that they would not.

Another limitation is that the bulk of published research to date applies to formal faculty development activities—to intentionally designed opportunities. The Tracer Project has gone one step further by looking at the results of those events, rather than merely at the often-contested value of the events themselves. Faculty professed to like events that had their priorities straight—meaning events that faculty perceived as focused on important aspects of teaching. They tended to dislike events that were required or that they perceived as addressing more trivial topics, such as learning to use the new course management software. Faculty valued initiatives that provided support and that were iterative in nature. The data from WSU and Carleton demonstrate that the more that faculty value the events offered, the more likely they are to attend and to apply what they have learned to their course syllabi and assignments.

This study does not fully explore the pathways of information into or out of a campus. Faculty live within both an institutional culture and a disciplinary culture. What role does the culture of the discipline, embodied in its professional societies and publication practices, play? When and how do institutional cultures and disciplinary cultures reinforce, contradict, or complement each other? The path is open for investigating the effects from attending disciplinary conferences, participating in residencies at the Carnegie Foundation, utilizing fellowships from other agencies, or taking advantage of the many other sources for development that are external to one's own institution. How do ideas travel among institutions? What are the effects of those ideas? Such questions need answers, and answers can come from a national conversation about effective teaching in higher education. Local data can address local concerns and contribute to a national conversation, and, in an era of widespread budget cuts, straitened circumstances, and attacks from both inside and outside higher education, such conversations are more necessary than ever.

As institutions look to join that conversation, or merely to provide evidence of teaching effectiveness on their own campuses, this research provides guidance in several ways:

- Begin by identifying as clearly as possible the goals for changes in instruction and by imagining clearly the role of faculty development in the change process. Note that this study does not address short-term or one-off events, since important changes do not happen that way. Instead, ask the question of how the one-offs (whether a WAC workshop or a session focused on learning the new classroom management system) can become part of the process of promoting a larger or higher-level goal. Think systematically about how each event, no matter its scope, contributes to others and to long-term goals. Think in terms of initiatives rather than single events.

- Similarly, identify the goals for learning by focusing on higher-order competencies. Look at competencies such as writing, thinking, teamwork, information literacy, or self-efficacy—the kinds of outcomes that are in institutions' formulations of outcomes for graduates. The more clearly an institution identifies these goals, and the more such goals are evident in every course of study, the more likely an initiative is to draw faculty commitment and to produce measurable change.

- Promote excellent teaching. Understand the enterprise of cultivating excellent teaching as systematic, not merely as a function of course evaluation. Foster a process of faculty learning that engages outside input, that supports reflective study of teaching practices, research into effects of changes in practice, and follow-up of further learning, change, and evaluation. Faculty who engage in the effort are pursuing good teaching. Some will become great teachers before others do, and some will always be better teachers than others, but all faculty will become better teachers than they were.

- Search for ways in which teaching and learning goals affect institutional practices that could count as routine faculty development. Orient those processes so that they support, identify, endorse, and promote improvements in teaching and learning. Realize that in most institutions, many of those practices may hamper the development of better teachers. Identify practices that are barriers and change them so that they encourage innovation in the classroom. Design systems so that they help overcome faculty members' reluctance or fear of exposing the inside of the classroom for an examination of their teaching practices. Performance reviews of all kinds must change from a punitive paradigm or a burdensome task to a set of practices that generate support for developing as a teacher.

- What educators want in students (higher learning) is what they want in faculty (learning about how to foster higher learning) and what they want in an institution (a context that supports higher learning for faculty and students). Expand the Direct Path model to a systems approach to institutional development. Higher education is a learning enterprise at all levels. A systems approach reveals the connections and interrelations among widely diverging occasions for learning, from introductory course work to grant-sponsored research, and from assessments of incoming students to accreditation studies focused on student learning outcomes. In a systems approach, institutional culture promotes and rewards improvement.

- The pathways to building a productive culture of teaching and learning on campus differ from one school to the next. Mount a search that can identify existing and potential pathways. Exploit existing pathways first, and design new pathways with research questions in mind. Collect data based on what current goals require, and do so with a sound research methodology. Plan an investigation that focuses on improving teaching, and allow the results to address institutional needs for accountability. Don't let the accountability need dominate the more important need for continuous improvement of teaching and learning. In assessment, every exit is an entry. Plan through the present evaluation toward future ones. Focus on process rather than more limited products.

- Think globally, act locally, and then act globally. Results from local efforts must reach to and beyond the scholarly commons. The most important audiences for improving teaching and learning are within the enterprise of higher education, but the audiences outside still matter greatly. Out there, common assumptions and perceptions are often oversimplified and rarely accurate—but only well-articulated, data-driven findings can counteract them. Again, a systems approach to such explorations can reach beyond the boundaries of higher education to society at large.

To build a productive culture of teaching and learning within an institution is to maximize the ability of faculty to learn and students to learn. This interaction lies at the heart of institutions of higher education. It is because faculty learning and student learning are intertwined that institutions foster and support the scholarly work of faculty. This study shows that these interactions are no less profound when applied to the process of teaching and learning than they are when thinking about disciplinary content and practices. Making visible the substantial faculty learning taking place and the culture that supports its impact will start to address criticism that higher education in America has lost its way. However, the most powerful response will be to build on this substantial base, thereby strengthening opportunities for faculty to learn about teaching and learning, and maximizing the potential for this knowledge to be shared across campus among faculty, students, and staff in a culture that values and sustains improvements in learning for all.

Afterword: Afterward

Richard Haswell

AFTER *FACULTY DEVELOPMENT and Student Learning*, what comes next?

My modest Colorado town bears the brazen motto "Gateway to All Season Fun." Del Norte (pop. 1,655) exhibits the metaphor *gateway* as an enabling fiction, of a breed with other "gateways" around the United States. They each boast that only through here can you reach wherever. They also lay a risky bet that people will not notice how *gateway* demotes the now and promotes the afterward. It seems to say, "Head out of town, to the all-season fun." Who wants to spend the night under a gate?

Or under an arch. Two decades ago, St. Louis, Missouri, "Gateway to the West," saw a pioneering venture to document the afterward. Nothing could have been riskier. In 1978 the education department at the University of Missouri–St. Louis established their local National Writing Project. To no one's surprise they called it the Gateway Writing Project. Dedicated to faculty development in the schools and funded through the Elementary Secondary Educational Act of 1965, the project was launched with a five-week summer institute for area schoolteachers. The teachers sampled scholarship in the teaching of writing, kept reading journals, brainstormed papers, participated in editing groups, and learned new and jiffy ways to teach and evaluate student writing. Radically, the project directors were not satisfied with testing the participants at the end of the five weeks that summer. They wanted to know what would happen afterward. So during the ensuing school year, they garnered almost a thousand student papers from the beginning and end of courses. Half were composed by students of teachers who had attended the summer institute, the other half by students of teachers who had not. Did the summer faculty workshop generate distinctive student learning? As I said, a daring and risky question.

One would think that the dare paid off when the findings showed seventh-grade students of trained teachers gaining more on a holistic score of their essays. But the risk bit back: findings also showed no significant difference in scores with sixth graders, where in fact, on average, students of non-trained teachers performed better. And in the error count—this was 1978, after all—the best the researcher could say is that students of trained teachers showed "as much improvement on most editing skills" as did other students (Shook 1981, 284). A forgettable piece of research, perhaps. Applying dubious and now outdated research methods, the study presents findings that lack much conviction. The iconoclastic nature of the study, however, should be remembered. In the field of college writing instruction, the effort to link teacher development with student learning was not repeated for decades.

In higher education there never has been anything comparable to the National Writing Projects of the schools. College faculty development projects, of course, have burgeoned with attempts to validate them. The validation, however, has taken the form of "one-off events," to accept the phrase offered here in chapter 7. Faculty participants are assessed *one* time at the end of the project and then everybody, including the project directors, takes *off*. Forget the afterward.[1] In post-secondary studies of writing across the curriculum, rare are the efforts to see if faculty development projects influence later faculty teaching. What's more, efforts to see if such projects improve student learning down the road don't exist.

Until this volume.

In findings that may startle a fair portion of the post-secondary world, this book demonstrates that faculty development projects do not end with the project. The events described here are not one-off; they are ever-on or ever-after. The gateway stands not at the project's start but at its end. These teachers at Carleton College and Washington State University have continued to apply and modify what they learned, as long as ten years later and no telling how much longer. And lo and behold, their students benefitted.

The implications of such findings run very deep. So, again, what may be the afterward of *Faculty Development and Student Learning*?

For me, the happiest reach will be, perforce, a truer representation of college faculty as teachers. The faculty studied here, year after year, course after course, worked to improve their teaching. And this was true of nearly all of them, whether preferring to attend more or fewer faculty development functions, whether working at a large research university or a small teaching college. Throughout higher education, says chapter 1, innovation and improvement in teaching are "almost a universal motivation." I taught college students full-time for forty-three years and not once did I enter a classroom without plans to teach that class period better than the time before. This volume persuades me, as if I didn't already know it, that my colleagues were doing the same. As long as it is read, the research will challenge the popular myth that post-secondary faculty are not "primarily interested in undergraduate student academic growth" (Arum and Roksa 2011, 125). It will show the myth as not only a fiction but a disabling fiction, because it will show it as a falsehood.

The myth shadows another. Supposedly, higher-education faculty focus on lower-level proficiencies. College teachers test only factual accuracy, the gossip goes, or respond to papers only with something like the Gateway Writing Project's "error count." This enabling fiction is seriously disabled by this book. Its documentation will speak for a long time. Again, both at a large public research institution, Washington State University, and at a small private liberal arts school, Carleton College, what energized and continues to energize the faculty are "higher-order competencies"— "writing, thinking, teamwork, information literacy, self-efficacy" (chapter 7). Actually, *higher* and *lower* are metaphors that may mislead. In these chapters, the teachers are searching rather for ways to get students *below* surface ideas, to those deep-sea depths where land-altering currents such as critical thinking and quantitative reasoning flow.

If college faculty navigate at these depths, how to study and measure teaching and learning? In the answer may lie this book's longest-lasting impact. *Faculty Development and Student Learning* argues that the old variables and methods won't be sufficient, such as faculty answering Likert items on the last day of the workshop, or students suffering through an AP subject exam in their senior year of college. Study of that wily, boundless interaction among students and teachers will have to be, these authors say, longitudinal, accumulative, and generative. Study of something that seems as one-off as a faculty reading of student portfolios will have to treat that reading as ever-after. Researchers will have to go after everduring "contagion effects" (chapter 5). It may sound daunting, but this book, simply by its own example, silences the common misreport that such effects are too chaotic or elusive to be located or described.

What is easily located and described, as we all know, is the massive resistance to afterward thinking in higher education. Across the land, by history, structure, and ideology, institutions are more conservative than progressive, more reactive than proactive, more Ondt than Gracehoper, more once-only than ever-after. Institutional bureaucracy sets the agenda. Course syllabi must be published before courses start, heads counted before teachers hired, seats fixed before class size judged, attendance kept before judging of students begins, final grades averaged before teachers rehired, tenure given before teacher ability shown. And before anything and everything, the bottom line has to be drawn. A teaching and learning center, devoted to student persistence and even life-long learning, is axed to end the fiscal year in the black. Alumns are followed solely to pry more money out of them. This pull of colleges and universities toward the short term should make us appreciate the courage and energy it took for the researchers whose work is presented between these covers to push back. Think of the odds against their kind of open-ended, fluid, long-term studies happening inside institutions whose primary concern, day in and day out, is getting their ducks in a row.

Ducks in a row? The metaphor may have originated with the midway duck pond where a line of plastic ducks floats by the carnival goer. But ducks, even artificial ones, don't naturally swim in a row. In 1992, a storm in the mid-Pacific split open a container on a cargo ship from Hong Kong and swept it overboard, releasing to wind and current some 28,000 plastic bathtub Floatees, including thousands of yellow ducks. Oceanographers were delighted. Since then they have been recording Floatee landfalls around the world. The giant currents that run below the ocean surfaces, it turns out, are not easy to measure. Floatees have helped to map the speed of the Subpolar Gyre that rotates between Japan and Alaska, and have made their way in floating ice as far as Maine and Scotland. Oceanographers, of course, had been conducting their own deep-sea current experiments long before 1992—a popular methodology was tossing overboard beer bottles containing messages—but the Floatee event was a windfall. Their method of study is called "tracer flow" (Ebbesmeyer 2005).

So this book's Tracer Project is well named. "Gateway," I now realize, is far too static an image for tracer studies. A clue is in the way institutional powers have captured the *gateway* image for their early-start and minority-start projects, which all too often serve, one-off-wise, only to get at-risk students duly enrolled and then to forget about them: Gateway Admissions, Gateway Program, Gateway Course, Gateway Scholarship, Summer Gateway, Gateway to Success. In a contrary direction, the Tracer Project envisions the university experience less like a land to be explored than an ocean with as yet uncharted currents beneath its ever-moving and ever-changing surfaces. Ideal tracer studies will take an educational event—constructed, natural, or even as serendipitous as a flock of plastic ducks lost at sea—and then track its complex flow. The studies can use anything as a tracer: a logical argument, a historical awareness, a numerical maneuver, a verbal phrase, a rhetorical arrangement, a social or psychological strategy. The key will be to prowl the flow however and how long it can be traced. That vision of teaching and learning research may turn out to be the furthest legacy of *Faculty Development and Student Learning*.

Acknowledgments

Even a project with five co-investigators and co-authors could not have been completed without the assistance of many additional people. Perhaps deserving of first mention are the good folks at the Spencer Foundation, whose generous funding enabled the research detailed in this volume. But even before that support, grants from FIPSE (at Washington State University and Carleton College) and the Bush Foundation (at Carleton) funded the long history of faculty development that made this project possible.

We must also acknowledge a great debt to Mary Huber, now retired from the Carnegie Foundation, who encouraged our early plans and over the past five years provided us with rich insights as a consultant to the project.

For their work at WSU, the authors especially thank Erin Mae Clark and Aaron Moe, who assisted in gathering data and analyzing the numbers; Beth Waddel, whose statistical acumen helped ensure that the analysis could stand up to scrutiny; and Dale Grauman, who spent endless hours in the library ferreting out studies that didn't do what we were claiming they didn't do. And to Charles Radcliffe, many thanks for manuscript preparation and for finding in earlier drafts all the places where we had repeated ourselves, often several chapters apart. In the very early stages of this project, Liz Hamp-Lyons visited WSU to help contextualize and design the procedures. And the long history of faculty development at WSU owes a huge debt to Gary Brown and others who labored at the now-defunct Center for Teaching, Learning, and Technology.

Carleton's former dean Scott Bierman intervened on our behalf with the Spencer Foundation, and the current dean, Beverly Nagel, has actively supported the project and encouraged its completion. We also thank the many faculty, staff, and administrative participants at both Carleton and WSU who laid bare for us their development histories, their views about teaching and learning, their institutional knowledge and practices, and their classrooms, and who participated as raters, providing the statistical and qualitative analyses that helped demonstrate our conclusions.

Finally, all of us are grateful to our families, whose support helped us throughout the project and without whom such endeavors would make little sense.

Thank you all.

Appendix 1. Guide to Rating Critical Thinking

Washington State University, 2001

1) Identifies and summarizes the **problem/question at issue** (and/or the source's position).

Scant	*Substantially Developed*
Does not identify and summarize the problem, is confused or identifies a different and inappropriate problem.	Identifies the main problem and subsidiary, embedded, or implicit aspects of the problem, and identifies them, clearly addressing their relationships to each other.
Does not identify or is confused by the issue, or represents the issue inaccurately.	Identifies not only the basics of the issue, but recognizes nuances of the issue.

2) Identifies and presents the <u>STUDENT'S OWN</u> **perspective and position** as it is important to the analysis of the issue.

Scant	*Substantially Developed*
Addresses a single source or view of the argument and fails to clarify the established or presented position relative to one's own. Fails to establish other critical distinctions.	Identifies, appropriately, one's own position on the issue, drawing support from experience, and information not available from *assigned* sources.

3) Identifies and considers <u>OTHER</u> salient **perspectives and positions** that are important to the analysis of the issue.

Scant	*Substantially Developed*
Deals only with a single perspective and fails to discuss other possible perspectives, especially those salient to the issue.	Addresses perspectives noted previously, and additional diverse perspectives drawn from outside information.

4) Identifies and assesses the key **assumptions**.

Scant	*Substantially Developed*
Does not surface the assumptions and ethical issues that underlie the issue, or does so superficially.	Identifies and addresses the validity of the key assumptions and ethical dimensions that underlie the issue.

5) Identifies and assesses the **quality of supporting data/evidence** and provides additional data/evidence related to the issue.

Scant	*Substantially Developed*
Merely repeats information provided, taking it as truth, or denies evidence without adequate justification.	Examines the evidence and source of evidence; questions its accuracy, precision, relevance, completeness.
Confuses associations and correlations with cause and effect.	Observes cause and effect and addresses existing or potential consequences.
Does not distinguish between fact, opinion, and value judgments.	Clearly distinguishes between fact and opinion, and acknowledges value judgments.

6) Identifies and considers the influence of the **context** on the issue.

Scant	*Substantially Developed*
Discusses the problem only in egocentric or sociocentric terms. Does not present the problem as having connections to other contexts—cultural, political, etc.	Analyzes the issue with a clear sense of scope and context, including an **assessment of the audience** of the analysis. Considers other pertinent contexts.

7) Identifies and assesses **conclusions, implications, and consequences**.

Scant	*Substantially Developed*
Fails to identify conclusions, implications, and consequences of the issue or the key relationships between the other elements of the problem, such as context, implications, assumptions, or data and evidence.	Identifies and discusses conclusions, implications, and consequences considering context, assumptions, data, and evidence. Objectively reflects upon their own assertions.

Contexts for consideration

Cultural/social
Group, national, ethnic behavior/ attitude

Scientific
Conceptual, basic science, scientific method

Educational
Schooling, formal training

Economic
Trade, business concerns, costs

Technological
Applied science, engineering

Ethical
Values

Political
Organizational or governmental

Personal Experience
Personal observation, informal character

© 2001 The Center for Teaching, Learning, Technology, General Education & The Writing Programs. Washington State University

Appendix 2. Methodologies in the Study at Carleton

RESEARCH METHOD	TYPE OF MATERIAL AND SCALE	PURPOSE
Artifact Study	Quantitative and Qualitative data: *Campus scale*	• Faculty teaching practices • Faculty implementation of faculty development in assignments
Interviews—80 individuals from 2009–2011	Qualitative data: *Individual cases* (approx. 21% of faculty)	• Range and styles of student writing • Student writing in response to assignments • Motivation to participate in faculty development • How/why faculty implement new learning in their teaching • Perceptions about effects of faculty development on teaching and on student learning • Institutional culture (context) • Faculty teaching experience/ practices at Carleton and previously (context)
Participant Observations —including a study of five freshmen seminar courses in Fall 2010	Qualitative data: *Individual cases* (approx. 60% of all faculty development opportunities from 2009–2011 and 33% of the in-class time for case study courses)	• Faculty experiences of faculty development • Content and skills taught in faculty development • Classroom teaching and learning practices • Classroom dynamics among students and teachers • Institutional culture (context)

RESEARCH METHOD	TYPE OF MATERIAL AND SCALE	PURPOSE
End-of-Workshop Surveys	Qualitative and Quantitative data: *Campus scale* (In 11 workshops from 2009–2011, 316 faculty and staff workshop attendees, 70% response rate overall)	• Motivations to participate in faculty development • Perceptions about workshop benefits and experiences (social networking as well as learning) • Plans for integrating new learning in teaching and research • Institutional culture (context)
Campus Surveys	Quantitative data: *Campus scale* (2010–2011 HERI survey, 59% response rate of instructional faculty)	• Participation in faculty development • Teaching practices related to faculty development • Institutional culture (context)
Faculty Development Participation Lists	Quantitative data: *Campus scale*	• Numbers and demographics of participants • Institutional culture (context)
Student Interviews and Surveys	Qualitative data: *Individual cases*	• Student views about teaching practices promoted by faculty development • Student life and approaches to learning (context)

Appendix 3. History of the Critical Thinking Rubric

THE ORIGINAL CRITICAL Thinking Rubric began as a project in Condon's graduate-level assessment seminar in 1997, when two students worked with the General Education Committee to devise a rubric that could measure changes (if any) in the ways students thought about the environment between the first year and mid-career (in partial evaluation of the effects of a grant from Weyerhauser, a prominent foundation in the state of Washington). That crude rubric showed enough promise that the Center for Teaching, Learning, and Technology (CTLT) headed up a working group (with participation from the Writing Programs and General Education) to refine it further. The goal at that point was to develop a rubric that could assess critical thinking. The group distilled fifty-five dimensions of critical thinking from the scholarly literature. Fifty-five dimensions were too many to assess practically or economically, so CTLT proceeded to test them in various assessment trials—located principally at colleges and universities around the state of Washington, but extending nationally and internationally as well. The resulting data, subjected to an ANOVA process, distilled the dimensions to the seventeen that mattered most within the academic community. Seventeen were still too many to assess efficiently or economically, so the data were further analyzed to find what correlations might exist among ratings of the seventeen dimensions. The hope was that assessing one dimension that correlated highly with another would allow for enough efficiency to make larger-scale assessments practical. The correlation study further reduced the list of dimensions to seven—small enough for a practical rating process on the scale of the institution, yet still sufficiently fine-grained to provide useful assessments of students' learning outcomes.

Appendix 4. Rating Forms

Assignment Rating Form (After Haswell 1988, see Willett, Iverson, Rutz, and Manduca 2014)

RATER ID: _____

	PAPER ID: _____			PAPER ID: _____				
	Greatly better	Obviously better	A Little better	Greatly better	Obviously better	A Little better	About the same	Not applicable
1. Provides opportunity to develop earlier assignments into a final product								
2. Provides opportunity for feedback and revision								
3. Gives guidelines for grading that are clearly articulated (and for acceptable writing)								
4. Articulates learning goals of the assignment clearly								
5. Elicits higher order thinking and writing: For example: • Asks student to develop an argument, hypothesis, or position • Requires student to write with a particular audience in mind • Asks student to identify and assess conclusions, implications, and consequences								
6. Prompts for effective use of data/evidence or quantitative reasoning								
7. Prompts for effective use of visuals								
8. Prompts for students to differentiate correlation from causation.								
Which assignment is better overall?								

Student Paper Rating Form (After Haswell 1988, see Willett, Iverson, Rutz, and Manduca 2014)

RATER ID: _____   PAPER ID: _____   PAPER ID: _____

	Greatly better	Obviously better	A Little better	Greatly better	Obviously better	A Little better	About the same	Not applicable
1. Demonstrates communication through clear language, effective writing mechanics, and strong organization								
2. Develops and presents an argument, hypothesis, or position								
3. Demonstrates a clear sense of the intended audience through literary devices, presentation of data, or voice								
4. Supports argument with appropriate data/evidence (includes citations)								
5. Uses precise language when addressing quantitative argument or data (avoids weasel words)								
6. Differentiates correlation from causation								
7. Makes use of visual representations within the text								
8. Identifies and assesses conclusions, implications, and consequences.								
9. Demonstrates higher level thinking in terms of analysis, synthesis, integrative, or evaluative thinking								
10. Includes the student's own point of view								
Which paper is better overall?								

Notes

FOREWORD

1. This question is from a 2009 survey of campus leaders participating in the Institutional Leadership and Affiliates Program of the Carnegie Academy for the Scholarship of Teaching Learning. The instrument and results can be found in Hutchings, Huber, and Ciccone 2011, Appendix A, 128–152.

1. CONNECTING FACULTY LEARNING TO STUDENT LEARNING

1. Substantial efforts were already under way in Writing Across the Curriculum (WAC) dating back to the late 1970s (Condon and Rutz 2012); in how to teach chemistry and calculus, dating back to the mid-1980s (Spencer 1999; Ganter 2001); in fostering critical thinking abilities, dating back to the early 1980s (Ruggiero 1984; Condon and Kelly-Riley 2004); and many others.

2. SITES OF FACULTY LEARNING

1. The survey response rate was 59 percent or 138 of 234 possible instructional faculty at Carleton that year.

3. SEEKING THE EVIDENCE

1. Haswell required a sample of students to write a paper in response to a prompt at the beginning and end of a semester in which they attended an introductory writing course. Raters knew that they were reading papers by the same students, but they did not know which paper came first.

2. The voluntary nature of the rating at Carleton made it difficult to compute an IRR statistic. In an ideal situation, all the work would be rated by multiple coders and would be rated by the same set of coders (fully crossed design). Our study was forced by circumstance to use a combination of multiple coders and single coders. In addition, different student work was rated by different subsets of coders. The team attempted to counteract the limitations of the small, changing pool of raters who were volunteering limited time by having a training session where raters achieved a level of inter-rater reliability on a sample prior to beginning the rating session. Researchers were also looking for only a binary agreement (better or worse). Thus, while a Cohen's kappa could be technically computed, it would not meet all the assumptions of the statistical test.

4. FACULTY LEARNING APPLIED

1. Twelve of the WAC workshop faculty had also taken part in the Critical Thinking Project, so the rate of innovation among the WAC faculty may be somewhat inflated.

2. One particularly active rater at WSU recently retired, having rated 5,479 portfolios, for a grand total of 27,395 individual samples.

6. REACHING STUDENTS

1. Professor Basil's assignments proved difficult to compare in a short time period, due to their overall length.

AFTERWORD

1. It seems *one-off* first appeared in the British foundry business around 1930. The phrase referred to a piece made once and never made again. *One* medallion might be struck *off* and then the die destroyed. Now we speak of *one-off* investment rollovers, *one-off* entertainment appearances, *one-off* gown creations, and so on. With some justification, William Safire (2007) argues that *one-off* is popular because nowadays people hesitate to say "unique."

References

Alliger, G. M., S. I. Tannenbaum, W. Bennett, H. Traver, and A. Shotland. 1997. "A Meta-Analysis of the Relations among Training Criteria." *Personnel Psychology* 50 (2): 341–358.

Angelo, T., and P. Cross. 1993. *Classroom Assessment Techniques: A Handbook for College Teachers.* Hoboken, NJ: Jossey-Bass.

Arum, R., and J. Roksa. 2011. *Academically Adrift: Limited Learning on College Campuses.* Chicago: University of Chicago Press.

Austin, A. E., M. R. Connolly, and C. L. Colbeck. 2008. "Strategies for Preparing Integrated Faculty: The Center for The Integration of Research, Teaching, and Learning." *New Directions for Teaching and Learning* 113: 69–81.

Bergquist, W. H. 1992. *The Four Cultures of the Academy: Insights and Strategies for Improving Leadership for Collegiate Organizations.* San Francisco: Jossey-Bass.

Bernstein, D. J., J. Johnson, and K. Smith. 2000. "An Examination of the Implementation of Peer Review of Teaching." *New Directions for Teaching and Learning* 83: 73–86.

Beyer, C., E. Taylor, and G. Gillmore. 2013. *Inside the Undergraduate Teaching Experience: The University of Washington's Growth in Faculty Teaching Study.* Albany: State University of New York Press.

Borko, H. 2004. "Professional Development and Teacher Learning: Mapping the Terrain." *Educational Researcher* 33 (3): 3–15.

Bransford, J. D., A. L. Brown, and R. R. Cocking. 2000. *How People Learn: Brain, Mind, Experience, and School: Expanded Edition.* Washington, DC: National Academies Press.

Brooks, D. C., L. Marsh, K. Wilcox, and B. Cohen. 2011. "Beyond Satisfaction: Toward an Outcomes-Based, Procedural Model of Faculty Development Program Evaluation." *Journal of Faculty Development* 25 (3): 5–12.

Brown, G., T. Smith, and T. Henderson. 2007. "Student Perceptions of Assessment Efficacy in Online and Blended Classes." In *Blended Learning: Research Perspectives,* ed. A. Picciano and C. Dzuiban. Needham, MA: The Sloan Center for Online Education.

Budd, D. A., K. Van Der Hoeven Kraft, D. A. McConnell, and T. Vislova. 2013. "Characterizing Teaching in Introductory Geology Courses: Measuring Classroom Practices." *Journal of Geoscience Education* 61 (4): 461–475.

Bunce, D. M., K. Havanki, and J. VandenPlas. 2008. "A Theory-Based Evaluation of Pogil Workshops: Providing a Clearer Picture of Pogil Adoption." In *Process Oriented Guided Inquiry Learning,* ed. R. S. Moog and J. N. Spencer, 100–113. Washington, DC: American Chemical Society.

Chism, V. N. N., and B. Szabó. 1997. "How Faculty Development Programs Evaluate Their Services." *Journal of Staff, Program, and Organization Development* 15 (2): 55–62.

Cobb, P., and J. Bowers. 1999. "Cognitive and Situated Learning Perspectives in Theory and Practice." *Educational Researcher* 28 (2): 4–15.

Condon, W. 2009. "Looking Beyond Judging and Ranking: Writing Assessment as a Generative Practice." *Assessing Writing: An International Journal* 14 (3): 141–156.

Condon, W., and D. Kelly-Riley. 2004. "Assessing and Teaching What We Value: The Relationship between College-Level Writing and Critical Thinking Abilities." *Assessing Writing* 9: 56–75.

Condon, W., and G. Leonhardy. 2001. "The Cracks of Writing Assessment: Exploring the Difficult Cases." In *Beyond Outcomes: Engaging Assessment with Instruction at a Large State University,* ed. R. Haswell. New York: Ablex.

Condon, W., and C. Rutz. 2012. "A Taxonomy of Writing Across the Curriculum Programs: Evolving to Serve Broader Agendas." *College Composition and Communication* 64 (2): 357–382.

Connolly, M. R., and S. B. Millar. 2006. "Using Workshops to Improve Instruction in Stem Courses." *Metropolitan Universities* 17: 53–65.

Dancy, M., and C. Henderson. 2010. "Pedagogical Practices and Instructional Change of Physics Faculty." *American Journal of Physics* 78 (10): 1056–1063.

Delbanco, A. 2012. *College: What It Was, Is, and Should Be.* Princeton, NJ: Princeton University Press.

Denofrio, L. A., B. Russell, D. Lopatto, and Y. Lu. 2007. "Linking Student Interests to Science Curricula." *Science* 318: 1872–1873.

Desimone, L. M. 2009. "Improving Impact Studies of Teachers' Professional Development: Toward Better Conceptualizations and Measures." *Educational Researcher* 38 (3): 181–199.

Eagan, M. K., E. B. Stolzenberg, J. Berdan Lozano, M. C. Aragon, M. R. Suchard, and S. Hurtado. 2014.*Undergraduate Teaching Faculty: The 2013-2014 Heri Faculty Survey.* Los Angeles: Higher Education Research Institute, UCLA.

Ebbesmeyer, C. C. 2005. "Beachcombing Science from Bath Toys." *Beachcombers' Alert.* http://beachcombersalert.org/rubberduckies.html. Retrieved October 23, 2014.

Ebert-May, D., J. Batlzi, and E. P. Weber. 2006. "Designing Research to Investigate Student Learning." *Frontiers in Ecology and the Environment* 4 (4): 218–219.

Ebert-May, D., T. Derting, J. Hodder, J. L. Momsen, T. M. Long, and S. E. Jardeleza. 2011. "What We Say Is Not What We Do: Effective Evaluation of Faculty Professional Development Programs." *Bioscience* 61 (7): 550–558.

Fairweather, J., and A. Beach. 2002. "Variations in Faculty Work at Research Universities: Implications for State and Institutional Policy." *Review of Higher Education* 26 (1): 97–115.

Felder, R. M., and R. Brent. 2010. "The National Effective Teaching Institute: Assessment of Impact and Implications for Faculty Development." *Journal of Engineering Education* 99 (2): 121–134.

Felten, P. 2013. "Principles of Good Practice in the Scholarship of Teaching and Learning." *Teaching and Learning Inquiry* 1 (1): 122–123.

Fisher, J. B., J. B. Schumaker, J. Culbertson, and D. D. Deshler. 2010. "Effects of a Computerized Professional Development Program on Teacher and Student Outcomes." *Journal of Teacher Education* 61: 301–312.

Fishman, B. J., R. W. Marx, S. Best, and R. T. Tal. 2003. "Linking Teacher and Student Learning to Improve Professional Development in Systemic Reform." *Teaching and Teacher Education* 19: 643–658.

Freeman, S., S. L. Eddy, M. McDonough, M. K. Smith, N. Okoroafor, H. Jordt, and M. P. Wenderoth. 2014. "Active Learning Increases Student Performance in Science, Engineering, and Mathematics." *Proceedings of the National Academy of Sciences* 111 (23): 8410–8415.

Fullan, M. 2001. *The New Meaning of Educational Change.* 3rd ed. New York: Teachers College Press.

Ganter, S. L. 2001. "Changing Calculus." *A Report on Evaluation Efforts and National Impact from 1988 to 1998.* Mathematical Association of America.

Garet, M. S., A. C. Porter, L. Desimone, B. F. Birman, and K. S. Yoon. 2001. "What Makes Professional Development Effective? Results from a National Sample of Teachers." *American Educational Research Journal* 38 (4): 915–945.

Gibbs, G., and M. Coffey. 2004. "The Impact of Training of University Teachers on Their Teaching Skills, Their Approach to Teaching and the Approach to Learning of Their Students." *Active Learning in Higher Education* 5 (1): 87–100.

Greene, J. C., V. J. Caracelli, and W. F. Graham. 1989. "Toward a Conceptual Framework for Mixed-Method Evaluation Designs." *Educational Evaluation and Policy Analysis* 11 (3): 255–274.

Hagay, G., and A. Baram-Tsabari. 2011. "A Shadow Curriculum: Incorporating Students' Interests into the Formal Biology Curriculum." *Research in Science Education* 41 (5): 611–634.

Hake, R. 1998. "Interactive-Engagement vs. Traditional Methods: A Six-Thousand-Student Survey of Mechanics Test Data for Introductory Physics Courses." *American Journal of Physics* 66: 64–74.

Hamp-Lyons, L., and W. Condon. 2000. *Assessing the Portfolio: Principles for Practice, Theory, and Research.* Cresskill, NJ: Hampton Press.

Handelsman, J., D. Ebert-May, R. Beichner, P. Bruns, A. Chang, R. L. Dehaan, . . . and W. B. Wood. 2004. "Scientific Teaching." *Science* 304: 521–522.

Haswell, R. 1988. *Contrasting Ways to Appraise Improvement in a Writing Course: Paired Comparison and Holistic.* Retrieved from ERIC Database. Ed294215.

———. 1991. *Gaining Ground in College Writing: Tales of Development and Interpretation.* Dallas: Southern Methodist University Press.

———. 2000. "Documenting Improvement in College Writing: A Longitudinal Approach." *Written Communication* 17 (3): 307–352.

———. 2001. *Beyond Outcomes: Assessment and Instruction within a University Writing Program.* Westport, CT: Greenwood.

———. 2012. "Methodologically Adrift." *College Composition and Communication* 63 (3): 487–491.

Henderson, C., A. Beach, and N. Finkelstein. 2011. "Facilitating Change in Undergraduate Stem Instructional Practices: An Analytic Review of the Literature." *Journal of Research in Science Teaching* 48 (8): 952–984.

Henderson, C., M. Dancy, and M. Niewiadomska-Bugaj. 2012. "Use of Research-Based Instructional Strategies in Introductory Physics: Where Do Faculty Leave the Innovation-Decision Process?" *Physics Education Research* 8 (2): 020104.

Hidi, S., and K. A. Renninger. 2006. "The Four-Phase Model of Interest Development." *Educational Psychologist* 41 (2): 111–127.

Hilbert, J., H. Preskill, and D. Russ-Eft. 1997. "Evaluating Training." In *Assessment, Development, and Measurement*, ed. L. J. Bassi and D. F. Russ-Eft, 109–150. Alexandria, VA: American Society for Training and Development.

Hoellwarth, C., M. J. Moelter, and R. D. Knight. 2005. "A Direct Comparison of Conceptual Learning and Problem Solving Ability in Traditional and Studio Style Classrooms." *American Journal of Physics* 73 (5): 459–463.

Hubball, H., and A. Clarke. 2010. "Diverse Methodological Approaches and Considerations for SoTL in Higher Education." *Canadian Journal for the Scholarship of Teaching and Learning* 1 (1): Article 2. http://ir.lib.uwo.ca/cjsotl_rcacea/vol1/iss1/2.

Huber, M. T. 2006. "Disciplines, Pedagogy, and Inquiry-Based Learning about Teaching." *New Directions for Teaching and Learning* 107 (Fall 2006).

Huber, M. T., and P. Hutchings. 2005. *The Advancement of Learning: Building the Teaching Commons.* San Francisco: Jossey-Bass.

Hurtado, S., K. Eagan, J. H. Pryor, H. Whang, and S. Tran. 2012. "Undergraduate Teaching Faculty: The 2010–2011 Heri Faculty Survey." Los Angeles: Higher Education Research Institute, UCLA.

Hutchings, P., M. T. Huber, and A. Ciccone. 2011. *The Scholarship of Teaching and Learning Reconsidered: Institutional Integration and Impact.* San Francisco: Jossey-Bass.

Johnson, D. W., R. T. Johnson, and E. J. Holubec. 1998. *Cooperation in the Classroom.* Edina, MN: Interaction Book Company.

Keeling, R. A., and R. P. Hersh. 2012. *We Are Losing Our Minds: Rethinking American Higher Education.* New York: Palgrave Macmillan.

Kelly-Riley, D., G. Brown, B. Condon, and R. Law. 2001. Unpublished Report. Pullman: Washington State University Critical Thinking Project.

Kember, D. 2002. "Long-Term Outcomes of Educational Action Research." *Educational Action Research* 10 (1): 83–103.

Kezar, A. J., and P. D. Eckel. 2002. "The Effect of Institutional Culture on Change Strategies in Higher Education: Universal Principles or Culturally Responsive Concepts?" *Journal of Higher Education* 73 (4): 435–460.

Kirkpatrick, D. L. 1959. "Techniques for Evaluating Programs." *Journal of the American Society of Training Directors (Training and Development Journal)* 13 (11): 3–9.

———. 2010. "The Four Levels Are Still Relevant." *T + D* 64 (9): 16.

Kuh, G. 2008. *High-Impact Educational Practices: What They Are, Who Has Access to Them, and Why They Matter.* Washington, DC: Association of American Colleges and Universities.

Laursen, S., A. B. Hunter, E. Seymour, H. Thiry, and G. Melton. 2010. *Undergraduate Research in the Sciences: Engaging Students in Real Science.* San Francisco: Jossey-Bass.

Lave, J. 1988. *Cognition in Practice: Mind, Mathematics, and Culture in Everyday Life.* Cambridge: Cambridge University Press.

Lave, J., and E. Wenger. 1991. *Situated Learning: Legitimate Peripheral Participation.* Cambridge: Cambridge University Press.

Lea, M. L., and B. V. Street. 1998. Student Writing in Higher Education: An Academic Literacies Approach. *Studies in Higher Education* 23 (2): 157–172.

LeLoup, L., and S. Shull. 2002. "The President and Congress: Collaboration and Combat in National Policy Making." 2nd ed. New York: Pearson.

Light, R. J. 2001. *Making the Most of College: Students Speak Their Minds.* Cambridge, MA: Harvard University Press.

Loucks-Horsley, S., K. E. Stiles, S. E. Mundry, and N. B. Love. 2003. *Designing Professional Development for Teachers of Science and Mathematics.* 2nd ed. Thousand Oaks, CA: Corwin Press.

Manduca, C., E. Iverson, J. A. McLaughlin, and R. H. Macdonald. 2005. "Enhancing Your Teaching and Developing New Leadership: Impact of the On the Cutting Edge Professional Development Program." *Eos Trans.* Agu 86 (52): Fall Meeting Supplement, Abstract Ed45a-02.

Macdonald, H., C. Manduca, D. W. Mogk, and B. J. Tewksbury. 2004. "On the Cutting Edge: Improving Learning by Enhancing Teaching." *Invention and Impact: Building Excellence in Undergraduate Science, Technology, Engineering, and Mathematics (Stem) Education,* 381. Washington, DC: American Association for the Advancement of Science.

Mettetal, G. 2001. "The What, Why, and How of Classroom Action Research." *Journal of Scholarship of Teaching and Learning* 2 (1): 6–13.

Middlecamp, C. 2008. "Chemistry in Context: Evidence, Goals, and Gaps." Commissioned paper for *Promising Practices: Innovations in Undergraduate Stem Education,* Board of Science Education. Washington, DC: The National Academies.

Monroe, B. 2003. "Fostering Critical Engagement in Online Discussions: The Washington State University Study." *Washington Center for Improving the Quality of Undergraduate Education Newsletter,* 31–33.

Nagda, B. A., S. R. Gregerman, J. Jonides, W. von Hippel, and J. S. Lerner. 1998. "Undergraduate Student-Faculty Research Partnerships Affect Student Retention." *Review of Higher Education* 22 (1): 55–72.

Narum, J., and C. Manduca. 2012. "Workshops and Networks in Brainbridge." In *Leadership in Science and Technology: A Reference Handbook,* ed. W. Sims, 443–451. Thousand Oaks, CA: Sage.

Patton, M. Q. 2011. *Developmental Evaluation: Applying Complexity Concepts to Enhance Innovation and Use.* New York: Guilford Press.

Pfund, C., S. Miller, K. Brenner, P. Bruns, A. Chang, D. Ebert-May, . . . and J. Handelsman. 2009. "Summer Institute to Improve University Science Teaching." *Science* 324, 470–471.

Pressick-Kilborn, K., and R. Walker. 2002. "The Social Construction of Interest in a Learning Community." In *Research on Socio-Cultural Influences on Motivation and Learning,* ed. D. McInerney and S. V. Etten. Scottsdale, AZ: Information Age Publishing.

Provost's Fact Book. 2012. Unpublished report. Pullman: Washington State University Office of Institutional Research.

Putnam, R. T., and H. Borko. 2000. "What Do New Views of Knowledge and Thinking Have to Say about Research on Teacher Learning?" *Educational Researcher* 29 (1): 73–109.

Ruggiero, V. R. 1984. *The Art of Thinking: A Guide to Critical and Creative Thought.* New York: Harper and Row.

Russell, S. H., M. P. Hancock, and J. McCullough. 2007. "Benefits of Undergraduate Research Experiences." *Science* 316 (5824): 548–549.

Rutz, C., W. Condon, E. R. Iverson, C. A. Manduca, and G. Willett. 2012. "Faculty Development and Student Learning: What Is the Relationship?" *Change* 44 (3): 42–47.

Rutz, C., and N. Grawe. 2009. "Pairing WAC and Quantitative Reasoning through Portfolio Assessment and Faculty Development." *Across the Disciplines: A Journal of Language, Learning, and Academic Writing* 6. http://wac.colostate.com/ato/assessment/rutz-grawe.cfm

Rutz, C., and J. Lauer-Glebov. 2005. "Assessment and Innovation: One Darn Thing Leads to Another." *Assessing Writing* 10 (2): 80–99.

Sabagh, Z., and A. Saroyan. 2014. "Professors' Perceived Barriers and Incentives for Teaching Improvement." *International Education Research* 2 (3): 18–40.

Safire, W. 2007. "One-Off." *New York Times Magazine.* June 24. http://www.nytimes.com/2007/06/24/magazine/24wwln-safire-t.html. Retrieved October 23, 2014.

Shook, J. 1981. "The Gateway Writing Project: An Evaluation of Teachers Teaching Teachers to Write." *Research in the Teaching of English* 15 (3): 282–284.

Shulman, L. S. 1993. "Forum: Teaching as Community Property." *Change: The Magazine of Higher Learning* 25 (6): 6–7.

Singer, S. R., N. R. Nielsen, and H. A. Schweingruber. 2012. *Discipline-Based Education Research: Understanding and Improving Learning in Undergraduate Science and Education*. Washington, DC: National Academies Press.

Singer, S. R., and C. Rutz, eds. 2004. *Reflections on Learning as Teachers*. Northfield, MN: College City Publications.

Smith, B. 1978. "Campus-Wide Governance at Carleton College: Its Performance and Prospects." *Liberal Education* 64 (1): 12–43.

Smith, B., R. Dostal, E. P. Gerdes, P. T. Christiano, A. Steele, L. A. Rossbacher, P. B. Pipes, et al. 1996. "What You Should Know: An Open Letter to New Ph.D.'s: The Commonwealth Partnership." *Profession*, 79–81.

Sommers, N. 2006. "Across the Drafts." *College Composition and Communication* 58 (2): 248–257.

Spencer, J. N. 1999. "New Directions in Teaching Chemistry: A Philosophical and Pedagogical Basis." *Journal of Chemical Education* 76 (4): 566–569.

Sternglass, M. 1997. *Time to Know Them: A Longitudinal Study of Writing and Learning at the College Level*. New York: Routledge.

Tierney, W. G. 1997. "Organizational Socialization in Higher Education." *Journal of Higher Education* 68 (1): 1–16.

Voelker, D., and R. Martin. 2013. "Wisconsin Teaching Fellows & Scholars Program Assessment Project: Final Report." Office of Professional and Instructional Development, University of Wisconsin System. http://www.uwsa.edu/opid/WTFS%20Study-FINAL%20 REPORT-Aug-2013-with%20ABSTRACT%20&%20APPENDICES(3).pdf. Accessed October 27, 2014.

Washington State University Board of Regents. 2009. *Self-Study Report for Reaffirmation of Accreditation*. Pullman: Washington State University.

Wayne, A. J., K. S. Yoon, P. Zhu, S. Cronen, and M. S. Garet. 2008. "Experimenting with Teacher Professional Development: Motives and Methods." *Educational Researcher* 37 (8): 469–479.

Webster-Wright, A. 2009. "Reframing Professional Development through Understanding Authentic Professional Learning." *Review of Educational Research* 79 (2): 702–739.

Weimer, M. 2006. *Enhancing Scholarly Work on Teaching and Learning: Professional Literature That Makes a Difference*. San Francisco: Jossey-Bass.

Weiss, C. 2002. "What to Do until the Random Assigner Comes." In *Evidence Matters: Randomized Trials in Education Research*, ed. F. Mosteller and R. Boruch, 198–224. Washington, DC: Brookings Institute Press.

Willett, G. 2013. "Beyond Pedagogy: Community Feeling, Educational Development and Power in a U.S. Liberal Arts College." *Learning and Teaching: The International Journal of Higher Education in the Social Sciences (Latiss)* 6 (1): 47–71.

Willett, G., E. R. Iverson, C. Rutz, and C. A. Manduca. 2014. "Measures Matter: Evidence of Faculty Development Effects on Faculty and Student Learning." *Assessing Writing* 20, 19–36.

WILLIAM CONDON is Professor of English at Washington State University. He is co-author of *Writing the Information Superhighway* and *Assessing the Portfolio: Principles for Practice, Theory, and Research*.

ELLEN R. IVERSON is Director of Evaluation at the Science Education Resource Center at Carleton College.

CATHRYN A. MANDUCA is Director of the Science Education Resource Center at Carleton College.

CAROL RUTZ is Director of the Writing Program at Carleton College.

GUDRUN WILLETT is Project Director for the Tracer Project and an associate at Ethnoscapes Global, LLC.

CPSIA information can be obtained at www.ICGtesting.com
Printed in the USA
LVOW11*1605290216

477151LV00013B/155/P